T.

oi

Time

Robin Crow

Table of Contents

Forward

As a teacher who loves to write, I have spent the last six summers working on writing projects. I've completed three full-length movie scripts, which I continue to enter in contests. As summer approaches, I pray for inspiration and new ideas to write about. Two years ago, this idea of taking back the gift of time in our lives began to take root in my mind.

I look forward to my summer writing projects, but during the school year, I struggle with the busyness of life, and find myself always feeling defeated and incapable of accomplishing all that I need and want to do. I realized that most people I know seem to feel the same, so I began to contemplate why our abundant lives seem to constantly be in a battle with time. I decided I would study time management from a philosophical as well as spiritual point of view, and search for a way to understand time as the gift that God intended it to be.

The most unnerving thing about writing this type of book is the fear it will be presumed I am establishing myself as an authority on a topic. This is absolutely not the case. As soon as I dove into research, study, and writing, I realized that the learning was truly for me. Writing this book is simply me sharing this journey with others who may benefit from some of the same reflections.

In this book, I explore scientific ideas, but I am not a scientist. I offer psychological observations, but I am not a psychologist. I contemplate scriptures, but I am not a Bible scholar. I am simply a follower of Jesus and philosopher asking *why* and *what if* questions, with the sole purpose to go deeper in my relationship with God.

In my early years as a teacher, my school was learning a new approach to teaching literacy. It was a paradigm shift that deepened our understandings in many ways. Each year we became better teachers and our students made more gains. After a few years, some of the seasoned teachers mentored the newer teachers. But even the experienced teachers continued to refine their skills. We reinterpreted a Gertrude Stein quote to become one of the guiding principles of our new learning: *"There is no 'there' there."*

For us it meant that we never *arrive* at total mastery; We never arrive "there" because the learning *always* continues. After teaching for more than twenty years, I can humbly say that *I will never arrive* at a destination where there is nothing left to learn. This perspective applies beyond my professional knowledge, to my faith walk, and my spiritual understandings as well. If we follow Jesus, and seek heavenly wisdom, we will be growing until the day we die.

In addition to being life-long learners, I believe we need to be willing to acknowledge that we are all most likely wrong about at least some of our perspectives and understandings. In any church, group of people, or family, there will be some differences of theology, even if we are all followers of Jesus and believe the Bible is the inspiration of God. Anyone who thinks they are undoubtedly right about everything is a prideful fool.

I know inspiring Christians who have differing views on certain issues. God made us individuals and gave us intricate minds to reason and establish our views and beliefs. He loves us all, even though none of us can possibly be one hundred percent spot-on about everything. Maturity is when you admit you don't have all the answers. If we were fail-proof, we wouldn't need faith or grace.

So please take this book as a humble offering of my own journey. It offers no formulas or clever slogans, but simply prompts you to study, reflect, and take action as the Holy Spirit leads you. In this busy, crazy, world where time is a luxurious and precious gift, I thank you for your willingness to invest some of it in reading these words.

Tick Tock

There is a time for everything, and a season for every activity under heaven. Ecclesiastes 3:1

I have had an annoying, reoccurring dream. It varies a little, but I am always at some type of amusement park. I love thrill rides – the higher and faster the better. In the dream I have been waiting with anticipation in line for a very long time, and just as I get close to boarding the ride, the park closes for one reason or another. It's obvious to me that this dream represents my fear of running out of time before I reach my goals.

Time is such a paradox, either going too fast or too slow. We lament how life rushes by too fast as we watch our children grow up much too quickly. We find the years uncomfortably accelerating and leaving some of our goals and dreams a distant blur in the rearview mirror of our lives. Diametrically, time can also creep far too slow as we wait for the focus of our most desperate prayers and deepest dreams to manifest.

Why does time seem to be my constant enemy? Offensively it sneaks up behind me when I am unprepared. Defensively, it is always out of my reach, slipping over the distant horizon out of my view. How I long to conquer and control this enemy. I yearn to be able to speed it up to reach my goals and slow it down every time I look in the mirror. Then there are those moments when I would love to hit a pause button. Those times that are so perfect, the only thing corrupting the moment is the haunting awareness that it will not last long enough. Where did this "Time Monster" come from? *And God said, "Let there be light,*

*and there was light. God saw that the
light was good, and he separated the
light from the darkness. God called
the light "day" and the darkness he
called "night." And there was
evening and there was morning –
the first day.*

Oh yeah. God made time. The one who has no beginning and no end, decided for some reason that we needed this measuring stick of days, years, and lifetimes.

I decided to research God's relationship with time and quickly got in over my head. We read in scripture that with God, *...a day is like a thousand years, and a thousand years are like a day. (2 Peter 3:8, Psalms 90:4)* This reveals to us that God exists outside of time's dimension. He transcends it.

Our physical world has four space-time dimensions of length, width, height (depth), and time. The science of physics tells us that time only exists when matter exists; So we can conclude that when God created the universe, *time* began. Time is a precondition for change, and likewise, change of any kind, is evidence that time has passed. We also know scientifically that time is relative to density and velocity.

The Bible tells us God created everything in six days. How long were those days? I don't know. The density of matter expanding from the point of creation could mean that the first days of the universe were billions of years in our time reference point. I have friends who believe creation was a literal six days as we know them, and others who think these "days" were billions of years. I've never been hung up about the details concerning the creation of the universe. I believe God made everything, but who am I to think I know exactly how it happened or how long it took?

We tend to use time as boundaries. When we pray, we expect answers within a reasonable period of time or we think the prayers have not been answered. We forget God does not have these time boundaries. Once when I was praying for a friend to be healed, I struggled when she died, feeling like all my prayers had been ignored by God. One of her family members gave me a new perspective when he told me *"God chose to heal her in person."* My prayerful expectations had been based on a physical place and time. I began to realize she was healed outside of our bubble of time. Our reasoning is based only on what we understand, according to our place and time perspectives. God exists beyond our realm of understanding.

There are many interesting theories on God and time, and if you want to give your brain a workout – Google it. It's all very interesting and mind stretching, but for the purposes of this book, we only have to agree on one thing – God established *time* at creation, and all that he creates…*is good.*

Time was a gift to us – a way to know when to put work aside and rest. He provides a fresh start, a rebirth with each new sunrise. *His mercies are new every morning. (Lamentations 3:22,23)* A timeless God created time for our benefit. Why do we struggle so much with this gift?

Through the generations we have engineered a multitude of ways to save time. From the printing press, to cars, to microwaves and computers, our growing collection of thousands of inventions makes everything we do more time efficient. The most successful and sought after devices are ones that save us money or time. Yet we find more and more ways to fill our time and make even more demands on it.

The Biblical book of Ecclesiastes reveals that our conflicted dance with time has been contemplated before. There are various theories about who wrote the book of Ecclesiastes. Most think it was written by King Solomon, but others believe it could have been someone else. I will take the liberty of calling this ancient wise teacher Solomon.

This book of wisdom is a thought provoking reflection on

man's unrest with his own finitude. Though written long before the existence of many of the activities and demands that fill my life, Solomon seems to struggle with the limitations of a lifetime defined by the endpoints of birth and death.

He proclaims, *"Everything is meaningless,"* and he supports his conclusion with observations such as *"Generations come and go." (1:4)* and *"When I surveyed all that my hands had done and what I had toiled to achieve, everything was meaningless, a chasing after the winds." (1:11)* In Chapter 2 he continues to rant that all his work and achievements are meaningless. He says, *"I hated all the things I had toiled for under the sun, because I must leave them to the one who comes after me." (2:18)* Solomon seems to be contemplating his own mortality, and the futile worth of his life's efforts.

The word *meaningless*, used throughout the book of Ecclesiastes, comes from the Hebrew word *hebel*. Although it is commonly translated as *meaningless* or *vanity*, it literally translates into the word *vapor* or *breath*, a metaphor for something that is temporary or elusive to hold onto. Perhaps Solomon was not saying life has no value, but rather that it was fleeting.

I once heard someone say, "The more we know, the more we realize how much we don't know." Solomon strikes me as a man who knew how much he didn't know, and felt confined by the limitations of his lifetime. He states, *"With much wisdom comes much sorrow; the more knowledge, the more grief." (1:18)*

Last week I walked through a Barnes and Noble bookstore and I felt depressed. There are so many books out there I want to read. I thought of Solomon's words, *...the eye never has enough of seeing, nor the ear its fill of hearing. (1:8)* If I could read twelve hours every day, I wouldn't make a dent in the books I would like to read. And what kind of isolated life would that be? Wouldn't it be wiser for me to spend my time interacting with people and making a difference in the world? Now that thought reminds me of several social justice issues I would like to fight for, and the organizations I would love to volunteer with, *if I just had the time.*

Then there are the places I want to visit, and the people I want to meet. Whenever I think of all the things on my bucket list, the clock mockingly ticks louder and faster. Like the foolish hare racing the tortoise, I don't have a chance against the clock because it just... keeps... going....

My only hope is to pull out. Pull out of the race, step out of the boxing ring, raise the white flag of surrender. Time was never supposed to be my enemy. I made it into that. Time was given as a gift from God. I need to learn to embrace it moment by moment.

We sing songs and buy greeting cards about living in the moment, one day at a time. But how do we do it? Is it a pipe dream? Solomon tells us it is good to enjoy the days God gives us because as God keeps us occupied with joy, we will seldom reflect on the days of our life. *(5:18-20)*

I long to live in the present moment. What a freedom that would be - where time is passive. Imagine living each moment so fully that time can neither go too fast nor too slow. Imagine living so deliberately, that time loses its power over you. Imagine living each moment, not as a moment on your life's timeline, but as a moment in eternity. Solomon said *God has set eternity in the hearts of men; yet they cannot fathom what God has done from beginning to end.* (3:11)

In Ecclesiastes Chapter 3, we are taught there is a time for everything – a season for every activity under heaven:

A time to be born and a time to die,
A time to plant and a time to uproot,
A time to kill and a time to heal,
A time to tear down and a time to build,
A time to weep and a time to laugh,
A time to mourn and a time to dance,
A time to scatter stones and a time to gather them,
A time to embrace and a time to refrain,
A time to search and a time to give up,

7

A time to keep and a time to throw away,
A time to tear and a time to mend,
A time to be silent and a time to speak,
A time to love and a time to hate,
A time for war and a time for peace.

This gift of time has been given to us for many purposes. And it truly is a gift.

He has made everything beautiful in its time.

Though Solomon bemoans that we have little control over the events in life, he concludes that the solution is to enjoy life, love what you do and find joy in your very existence.

I know that there is nothing better for men than to be happy and do good while they live. That everyone may eat and drink, and find satisfaction in all his toil – this is the gift of God.

So, "Carpe Diem" – *Seize the Day.* He makes it sound so easy.

Group discussion questions:

1. When has time moved too fast for you? When has it moved too slow?

2. How do you perceive time when thinking about pursuing your goals? Do you have negative feelings about time?

3. Share one or two goals on your bucket list.

4. What does it mean to you to live one day at a time?

Read and discuss these scripture passages:

Genesis chapter 1

Ecclesiastes chapters 1 & 3

Timeless Truth

*Even to your old age and gray hairs
I am he, I am he who will sustain
you. I have made you and I will
carry you; I will sustain you and I
will rescue you. Isaiah 46:4*

We sometimes describe great works of art or literature as being *timeless*...meaning they are unaffected by the passage of time. We believe they are as beautiful or appreciated today as they were when they were first created. We would probably laugh if someone used this adjective to describe us, yet I think that is the way our Creator sees us: To him we are as beautiful now as in the very first moments of our design.

One of my favorite authors, Mitch Albom, wrote a book called *The Time Keeper*.[1] This very creative fable is about the first man on earth to find a way to count hours and measure time. The character in the story, Dor, invented the first sundial, then clock, then calendar. The consequences of his pursuit resulted in the misery of all those who thereafter became consumed by the counting of years, months, days, hours, and minutes. Dor, now renamed "Father Time," is banished to a cave, and suffers for thousands of years, forced to listen to the miserable voices of those who come after him, trapped in their obsessive measurement of time. He is given a chance to redeem himself by intervening in the lives of two people who need to learn the value of time.

It's an interesting premise, that the precious gift of time was irrevocably altered when we began to measure it. One of our human flaws is our insistence to measure and compare everything we are blessed with.

There is physical evidence that time has been measured throughout human history. Candle clocks, water clocks, and sun dials and sticks have been found in ancient civilizations throughout the world. The first mechanical clocks appeared in 14th century Europe. In 1577, the minute hand was invented solely for the purpose of an astronomy tool. *Try to imagine a time before minutes mattered.* The first formal calendars came from Mesopotamia over 5,000 years ago and were based on lunar cycles and planting seasons. Maybe I would feel more celebratory about approaching my 60th barley harvest.

Because we measure time, and categorize time units into days, months, and years, I have a number assigned to me referred to as my "age." There were a few years long ago when I remember wishing the number was higher. I wanted to be old enough to drive or date or drink a beer. But all too soon that perspective changes, and numbers that once seemed very high, now seem youthful. Our world makes laws, gives privilege, and often judges us based on how many trips we have made around the sun.

We can ignore the candles on the cake, but even if we surrendered our tradition of counting our years of existence, our very physiology is governed by biological clocks and circadian clocks that regulate our DNA and hormones in ways we are still understanding. Women experience these biological clocks in ways that are difficult to ignore. We know precisely when our season for childbearing has begun and when it ends. These innate, internal clocks are part of the grand design of our Creator. They are another mystery of the gift of time.

We tend to view this legacy of time as an enemy too. I can remember the first time I plucked a gray hair from my head. That hair represented a rogue, unwelcome outsider in my exclusionary society of strands. But I tried hard to believe the scripture that *"Gray hair is a crown of splendor." (Proverbs 16:31)* I now have a growing and integrated community on my multi-chromatic head, and I try to think of them as symbols of grace. My reckless teen years could have easily led to the end of my life, but instead, I have lived to see these gray hairs.

I also remember the first time I humbled myself and put on reading glasses. I looked in the mirror and suddenly every wrinkle on my forehead looked like the Grand Canyon. I frowned as I thought, maybe our vision weakens with age to a soft focus for a good reason. But if we truly believe every day is a gift, the signs of aging in our bodies are a testament to a cup that is running over.

It is easy to be discouraged by the effects of time on our bodies, but we have to remember that our bodies are just temporary homes for our souls.

I like the Message version of 2 Corinthians 5:1-5:

> *We know that when these bodies of ours are taken down like tents and folded away, they will be replaced by resurrection bodies in heaven— God-made, not handmade—and we'll never have to relocate our "tents" again. Sometimes we can hardly wait to move—and so we cry out in frustration. Compared to what's coming, living conditions around here seem like a stopover in an unfurnished shack, and we're tired of it! We've been given a glimpse of the real thing, our true home, our resurrection bodies! The Spirit of God whets our appetite by giving us a taste of what's ahead. He puts a little of heaven in our hearts so that we'll never settle for less.*

Our bodies have an expiration date. But our Maker has designed us that way, and he has something better waiting for us.

Perhaps some of you find your mind wandering off through this chapter because you are too young to think about gray hair or aging skin. Know that although many of us may be envious of your youth, we were once there too. I remember my misguided attitudes and perceptions of older people when I was younger.

One of the flaws of our Western Culture is that we glorify youth and pity the aged. Other cultures, including those in China, Greece, Japan, and Korea, honor and esteem their elders, holding elaborate celebrations when age milestones are reached. I challenge each of us to notice those around us who have been here the longest, and appreciate the beauty and wisdom that comes from time lived. Then go tell them how wonderful they are.

I believe that much of our skewed perception of aging is the result of the constant brainwashing we are exposed to concerning what makes one beautiful. We are a culture consumed by body image. We are bombarded with anti-aging products, weight loss solutions, plastic surgery, and a plethora of makeup and hair care products.

I am embarrassed to think how many times I have purchased something claiming to make my hair thicker or my skin smoother: My hair conditioner label states that it is "age-defying". The definition of defiance is: *Bold disobedience; resistance to authority; combative.* Does my conditioner really do all that?

Why are we so unsatisfied about how we look? Why are we prone to be so critical of ourselves and each other? My prayer is that we can look in the mirror and see the masterpiece that God created.

Your beauty should not come from
outward adornment, such as
elaborate hairstyles and the wearing
of gold jewelry or fine clothes.
Rather, it should be that of your
inner self, the unfading beauty of a

> *gentle and quiet spirit, which is of*
> *great worth in God's sight.*
> *1 Peter 3:3-4*

This is the beauty that grows with time. The longer we walk with our Lord, the more we know his character, and the greater our heart will align to his heart. Should we choose to focus on our inner beauty that is woven together from our spiritual DNA, or do we instead focus on the temporary beauty that has been unjustifiably defined by culture and people?

We sometimes let the physical aging of our bodies affect us psychologically. When I acknowledge my body is aging, my mind and my spirit want to follow suit. I start believing that I'm too old to do something, or it's safer to stay with the status quo. But if God continues to give me days to live in this world, I must have a purpose, and I cannot use excuses to waste this gift of time. *Philippians 1:6* tells us that we can be confident that he who began a good work in us will see it through to completion.

Psalms 92 is a beautiful Psalm of praise and thankfulness. In my Bible, I have highlighted the last verses, and they are a prayer of my heart. *(V 12-15)*

> *The righteous will flourish like a palm tree,*
> *they will grow like a cedar of Lebanon;*
> *planted in the house of the Lord,*
> *they will flourish in the courts of our God.*
> *They will still bear fruit in old age,*
> *they will stay fresh and green,*
> *proclaiming, "The Lord is upright;*
> *he is my rock, and there is no wickedness in him."*

My prayer is to bear fruit in old age. You are never too old to pursue your dreams. Currently, and throughout history, the world is full of people who have accomplished significant things later in life. I could easily write an entire chapter with these astonishing and inspirational stories.

One of my favorites is Kimani Maruge from Kenya. When his government announced free elementary education in 2003, He enrolled in first grade at the age of 84. He was determined to learn how to read, and he did. Later he flew on a plane for the first time to address the United Nations World Summit on the importance of free primary education. Maruge's dream took courage, humility, and faith. These qualities surpass the boundaries of clocks and calendars.

If you think you are too old to do something, someone out there has probably already proven you wrong. I suggest that you pause and Google this sentence: *Oldest person to* _____ (you fill in the blank). Whether you have dreamed of writing a book, running a marathon, climbing Mount Everest, or anything else you can imagine, you will most likely find someone who accomplished it in spite of their age.

And remember not every dream or goal is headline worthy. Every day around the earth, people step out of their comfort zones, and ignore the excuses of time's parameters to make a difference in some else's life. We can touch the lives around us with the fruits of the Holy Spirit: *love, joy, peace, forbearance, kindness, goodness, faithfulness, gentleness, and self-control. (Galatians 5:22-23)*

I want to receive the *finite* gift of time that is given to me, and invest it by living fully and blessing others, to honor the *infinite* one. Now there's a timeless idea.

Group discussion questions:

1. Do you think we are too driven by clocks and calendars? What does this look like in your life?

2. Do you make assumptions about people regarding their age? Do you ever feel people may be too young or too old for something?

3. How do you feel about the aging process? Do you look at accumulating years as a gift or a curse? How should we view aging?

4. How does our culture define beauty? Why? What do you think God considers beautiful?

5. Is there anything you feel you are too old to do? What does it mean to you to bear fruit in old age?

Read and discuss these scripture passages:
2 Corinthians 5: 1-10
Philippians 1:6
Psalms 92:12-15
Psalms 139:14-16
1 Peter 3:3-4
2 Corinthians 4:16-18

Blinks and Dashes

Our days may come to seventy years,
or eighty, if our strength endures; yet
the best of them are but trouble and
sorrow, for they quickly pass, and we
fly away. Psalms 90:10

This statistic hasn't changed much since this Psalm was written. The most recent figures I could find had an American man's life expectancy at 76.3 years and 81.2 years for a woman. We celebrate our birthdays marking another year that has passed in our life. Another year, a total of five hundred, twenty-five thousand, six hundred minutes.

How many times have we thought, where did the years go? Yet, we have thousands of memories and stories to answer that question. If we look at our life with a wide-angle lens, we may see a myriad of events, decisions and experiences, good times and bad. Like the colors in an impressionistic painting, these events blend together to paint the canvas of our life.

Hurting people, those living in pain or experiencing adversity, often feel trapped in time. The wide-angle lens has become a microscope. If you have experienced a tragedy or intense time of pain, you know this overwhelming feeling - nothing else matters. Time seems to stop. It's like those music videos where the singer is in slow motion while the world speeds around them in a blur. When we hurt deeply, we can feel offended that the rest of the world, and time, keeps going, untouched by our pain.

In my own conflicts with time, I try to console myself with what I call the *blink perspective*. I blink my eyes quickly and remember that compared to eternity – my entire life is less than that blink. Somehow it lightens the burden; helps me to step back from my extreme focus on the matter at hand. Maybe it just gets me thinking about eternity – a place of perfection with God and no pain or suffering. No more worries of time going too fast – it will never run out. No more worries of time going too slow – we will not be waiting or wanting for anything. The blink helps me remember that chaos and pain are temporary. It's humbling to accept that our lives are only a blink in eternal time.

But let's change our perspective for a moment. Like viewing our planet from outer space with Google Earth on our computer and clicking the zoom again and again until we see the backyard of our house, we are going to refocus from the blink of our lifespan in eternity to the span of time that falls between our birth date and death date. Some call it the "dash." The dash that is between those two dates on your grave marker. The dash symbolizes your life on this earth. It represents a lifetime of joys, sorrows, successes and achievements, mistakes and failures, people who have come and gone in our life, and memories good and bad.

When my Dad passed away, I reflected on his dash. The video collage they often show at memorial services is only a movie trailer of a life lived. My Dad's funeral video was a unique summary of his life with some childhood and army pictures, photos of him with our family, and clips of his church and ministry endeavors. The pictures rolled with the music of George Burns singing, *"I Wish I Was Eighteen Again,"* and Louis Armstrong's, *"It's a Wonderful World."* Text flew into the frames with annotations and sprinkles of humor. People chuckled as they realized my Dad had created his own funeral movie. He wanted to share how blessed his "dash" had been.

My Dad was a special man. I thank God often for blessing me with a Dad that taught me faith, generosity, and mercy. Along with a career as a teacher, coach, and principal, he taught Sunday School and Bible studies for over thirty years. He served in many ministry capacities, including a prison ministry. At his funeral service, many people shared touching stories of his impact on their lives. He was a simple man with a lot of love in his heart, and he lived his life well.

The Christmas after he died, I received cards and letters from some people he had ministered to in prison who had not heard the news of his passing. I wrote back to inform them of his death and later received two precious letters that I cherish dearly. The writers of these letters, still in prison, told of my Mom and Dad's impact on their lives. They wrote of feeling loved for the first time and referred to my parents as their first perceivable understanding of the love of Jesus. One woman said she was loved into wholeness as she described the legacy that resulted from my Dad sharing God's love. I realized that how he used the time of his dash had changed lives and had an impact that would continue into the future, and eternity.

A few weeks later, I found out that an old friend of mine had died alone in her apartment. I taught at the same school as Susan, years ago. When her mother died, she slipped deep into depression, and never climbed out. She became reclusive, and troubled by fears and loneliness. She fell out of contact with friends and though I visited her and tried to encourage her to pursue working again and stepping out socially, she was never able to do it. There wasn't even a funeral for Susan. There were no family or friends left to talk about her life.

My friends in my Bible study were gracious to join with me to honor Susan's memory by having our own little service. They had met her when I recruited them to help clean her apartment. I'm sure there is much in Susan's dash that I don't know. I know she must have impacted many children during her years as a teacher. But thinking about Susan's last lonely years makes me very sad. Her dash is mostly a mystery.

The loss of these two lives made me reflect on my own dash. Would I impact lives the way my Dad did? Or would I quietly pass from this life without being missed? The line that connects our birth to our death is truly best measured by how it intersects with other lives along the way. Think about the moments you have been lifted up by another human being. Think of those defining moments when someone impacted you and possibly even changed your life.

When my third grade teacher, Mrs. Ely, told me I was a great writer, it took only a few seconds for her to tell me. But I remember that moment to this day. At age eight, I believed I was a writer. Everyone we cross paths with has dash potential, and we may be the one to ignite it. When I work with students struggling to learn to read, I remind myself that they might be a future president or the next Einstein. Our life journey influences and is influenced by many other lives along the way.

A few years ago, I read Martin Luther's quote, *"If you want to change the world, pick up a pen and write,"* This is when I began to channel my passions into my writing. I had dreams of my script being made into a movie that would result in people becoming more compassionate to the homeless. I envisioned cities and churches working together for solutions, and organizations building housing and providing job training. I know the power of a good story to motivate, but I also know this is a big and improbable goal.

I haven't given up, and I refuse to believe I have wasted this time by writing. But I also know not all the dots on my timeline are going to be big important events. Maybe the letters I've written to a friend struggling with depression, or the thank you letter to the underappreciated volunteer will be the writing that really changes the world. The world changes one person at a time, and we all have the capability to make that happen.

The author of eternity provides us with an amount of time to live our lives on this earth. He gifted us with that dash, and also with free will – we determine how we spend the time in our life. We've all heard the quote, *"Live each day as if it were your last."* People have referenced it in speeches and sermons and many songs have been written about it. I imagine most of us agree with these words of wisdom, yet find putting them into practice somewhat elusive.

How we use our time would most likely change dramatically if we knew it was running out. When I think about my own "to do" list for today, nothing on it would seem very important anymore. If I have depressed you, I apologize. My intent is not for you to focus on the time you don't have, but rather to appreciate, embrace, and be a good steward of the gift of time you have been given.

All that we have belongs to God. He gives freely, yet longs for us to freely give back to him. We have learned this ancient truth with God's instruction on tithing our wealth *(Malachi 3:10-11)*, and from Jesus who taught us:

> *"Give, and it will be given to you. A good measure, pressed down, shaken together and running over, will be poured into your lap. For with the measure you use, it will be measured to you." – Luke 6:38*

Time is as much of a resource to us as money. We are blessed to receive it, and we decide how we spend it. If we give back to him what we received from him to begin with, I think we will have more than enough time….*good measure, pressed down, shaken together and running over.*

So how do I measure time? Do I count the number of years I have until retirement, the number of days until the weekend, the number of hours of sleep I need to be able to function at work, or the number of minutes I squeeze out for my morning devotions? All of these are part of my dash. When I contemplate my struggle with time management, it becomes painfully clear where my priorities are.

In the parable of the talents, *(Matthew 25:14-30)* Jesus teaches us God's expectations for the gifts he has blessed us with. Everyone has been entrusted with various resources of talents, time, and wealth, and we are responsible for using those resources to honor the one who gave them to us. The time given to us in our dash – our life on this earth, has been entrusted to us to invest wisely.

The gift of time in my life has been riddled with my own wasted detours and missed opportunities. Some of the wasted detours have been due to the things the world deems important, and some of the missed opportunities are due to things the world deems insignificant. I am still learning and growing. My hope and prayer is that when my time ends, I will hear him say, "Daughter, I am pleased".

I resolve to take back the gift of time and embrace whatever God gives me with gratitude. I resolve to surrender things that steal my time, and invest my time in ways that would please my Lord. I want my timeline to intersect with people and possibly help change the quality of their dash. I want my dash to honor and please the giver of time. Are you with me?

Group discussion questions:

1. Have you ever felt like you were trapped in time or time seemed to stop?

2. How do you contemplate the concept of a timeless eternity? How does the idea of never ending time make you feel?

3. How would you spend the last day of your life?

4. What do you want to happen within your dash?

5. Is time a resource we should give back to God? What does it look like to give God an offering of time?

6. How do we invest our gift of time? What do we invest it in?

Read and discuss these scripture passages:
Malachi 3:10-11
Luke 6:38
2 Corinthians 9:6-7
Matthew 25:14-30
James 4:14

Time stops for no man?

*...the sun stopped in the middle of
the day and delayed going down
about a full day. There has never
been a day like it before or since, a
day when the Lord listened to a man.
Surely the Lord was fighting for
Israel. – Joshua 10:12-14*

Joshua was a man with a big mission – to lead Israel into Canaan and claim it, fulfilling God's covenant to Abraham to provide this land to his descendants. *(Gen. 12)* A big mission requires big faith, and Joshua had it. It takes a gutsy man to pray to God to make the sun stand still.

After an all-night march, Joshua's army was set to battle the joined forces of five kings of the Amorites. Perhaps Joshua wanted his people to know without any doubt that God was leading them when he publicly prayed for the sun to stand still. *(Joshua 10)* In verses 12-14 it is clear that this convinced the Israelites that God was indeed with them.

Long before the known science of the earth's revolution around the sun, people perceived the sun rise up in the morning and then disappear in the evening. We still refer to sunrises and sunsets, even though we now know the sun isn't the one moving.

If you attempted to Google *God and Time,* and were slightly overwhelmed, the theories on the day the sun stopped for Joshua and the Israelites will serve as a brain deluge as well. From solar eclipses to refraction theory, there are arguments and debates for dozens of possible scenarios. I guess it's our human nature to want to explain everything miraculous that we don't understand. Some notable Bible scholars seem to believe the best explanation is that the rotation of the earth slowed down to about forty-eight hours instead of the normal twenty-four.

Another Bible story found in *2 Kings 20,* and again in *Isaiah 38,* tells of Hezekiah's plea to the Lord when facing death. Through the Prophet Isaiah, the Lord tells Hezekiah he will add fifteen years to his life. The Lord seals his promise with a sign and the sun's shadow cast on the stairway of Ahaz goes backward ten steps. *(Isaiah 38:7,8)* I'm sure scholars and scientists have theories on this phenomenon too. How God did it really doesn't matter. He created time, the earth, the sun, and the entire universe, so I think he can do whatever he wants with them, including making time stop or even reverse.

Are these ideas too radical to wrap your mind around? I'm writing this on July 3 and I just got a text from my friend Kenda who is on a mission trip to Thailand. Her text said "Happy 4th of July," because she flew forward in time as she traveled there. We can accept the things we can explain, but tend to reject the things we can't.

> *"For my thoughts are not your thoughts, neither are your ways my ways,"* declares the Lord. *"As the heavens are higher than the earth, so are my ways higher than your ways and my thoughts than your thoughts."* Isaiah 55:8-9

Believing God not only created, but governs and presides over time should help us surrender our claim to ownership. We treat time like a commodity that we can trade for treasure. We make choices every day with how we use this gift of time. Though we do not know how long the dash of our life will be, we have been given the free will to decide how to spend the time that has been allotted to us.

We often hear the quote from Ben Franklin, *"Time is money."* I think most people would agree with Franklin's conclusion. We use our time working to earn money, and we spend much of our money on things that will save us time, or make our time more enjoyable. I think many of us have an even tighter grip on our time than our money. We make daily decisions and judgements based on how much time something requires of us. Try to notice how often you hear someone say, *"I don't have time..."*

All that we have comes from God, including the time he gives us. He determines the time represented by the dash on our gravestone, and every day that he gives us is a gift. Have we wasted or misspent some of this time? Some of us have wasted years, and all of us probably waste minutes or even hours every day. But we are not going to get wrapped up in guilt or regret. God forgives us and every day is a new day.

So here I am, in my late-fifties, with plenty of unfulfilled dreams and goals, and I'm dreaming that the amusement park is going to close just as it's time to board the ride. I want to stop feeling threatened by time, and learn how to live each day in gratitude, while being a good steward of the time God has blessed me with. We know that God multiplies what is given back to him, so I resolve to return the gift of time back to him. If he can make time stop and even go in reverse, I believe he can supply me with all the time I need each day. I'm ready to stop being so selfish with my time.

I spend time with the Lord every day, often praying when I'm driving, taking a walk, or in the shower. But in all honesty, the shower holds me hostage from multitasking, and when I'm walking or in my car, most distractions are out of my reach. So I find that I pray mostly when I am unable to do anything else. I admit, if a text comes in on my phone when I'm praying, I stop and read it. Doesn't God deserve my undivided attention? I want to return the gift of time to my Lord in an uncompromising, and absolute way.

Remember how physics explains that time is an indicator of change? In our walk with God we are continually growing and striving to be more like Christ. I don't ever want to think that I have reached the ideal. Change means growth.

I have gone through many seasons of transformation and refining, and I continue to try to identify the roadblocks and distractions that hinder my relationship with God. Currently, I know I need to be a better steward of this gift of time he has given me.

I decided the first step was to analyze how I actually spend my time. If we really want to successfully change something, we have to study it first. We have all experienced casual commitments and resolutions that never take root. As I write this, I am on a thirty-day cleansing diet. To stay locked into it, I have to plan and write down each meal, so I stay focused on eating the right things. When I see my little food journal in the morning, I know I have made a plan I need to stick to.

I knew that if I wanted to change how I spend my time, and delegate more quality time to uncompromised communion with God, I would have to take a hard, honest look at what fills my hours. I decided I would carefully document how I spent my time for a couple of weeks. I knew this would be a journey with some difficult revelations, and frankly I was a little scared about what I would find, and the changes I would be induced to make. I invited the women in my small group to join me in this quest of analyzing how we spend our time. I value their support dearly, and I knew we would all learn from each other.

I am very blessed to have a group of Christian women that support me and pray for me as we grow closer to the Lord together. I am especially blessed by the honesty and transparency of these women. In a world where we are always expected to be capable and confident, it's a true blessing to have friends who you feel free to confess your struggles to. I have found that the path to growth best starts with a few steps of humility.

Growth journeys are hard to do alone. That's why we have successful organizations like Weight Watchers and Alcoholics Anonymous. Taking a hard look at how we spend our time, and reflecting on possible changes, requires an open mind and determined attitude.

I'll be the first to say that I'm just too busy to deal with time management. *A little humor helps too.* So feel free to band together with your own superhero team to defeat the villains who are holding time captive. We probably won't find a way to stop time or turn back the clock, but we can encourage each other and share wisdom and empathy.

Group discussion questions:

1. Do you think God is still able to stop or reverse time?

2. Is it harder for you to give of your time or your money?

3. Do you find it difficult to devote undivided time with God?

4. Are you willing to document how you spend your time so you can reflect and possibly make some changes?

Read and discuss these scripture passages:

Joshua 10:1-15

Hezekiah's prayer: 2 Kings 20:1-11

Isaiah 38:1-7

Shooting Stars and Four-Leaf clovers

Better one handful with tranquility
than two handfuls with toil and
chasing after the wind.
-Ecclesiastes 4:6

Before I gave my women's group the homework assignment of categorizing and recording all the ways they spend their time over a week, I nervously wondered how they would respond. Asking busy women to add another item to their *to do* list in the interest of being better managers of time, seemed absurd and irrational. But gracious women that they are, they agreed to give it a try. I provided a daily planner with the hours divided into fifteen-minute increments to record the activities that filled their days.

The next week, the discussion quickly focused on our revelation of how much we multitask. This made the recording of activities very difficult. Everyone noticed that they interwove activities so frequently, they really had no idea how much time something actually took them.

My friend Kenda said she was so determined to get an accurate measurement, she made herself fully complete a task before she went on to something else. She was pleased to discover she not only accomplished more, she also didn't have to search for her glasses and phone as much when she stayed focused on one task at a time.

As I contemplated our discussion and observations, I became increasingly more aware of the time I too spent divided between multiple activities. We take pride in our ability to do many things simultaneously, even highlighting our ability to multitask on our resumes. But let's call it what it really is – multitasking is really just juggling. Research has shown that we are actually switching our attention from task to task, and we have learned to do it extremely fast. But when we juggle, we are never really touching all of the balls in the same moment.

Neuroscientists have revealed they can actually see the brain struggle as it attempts to multitask, demonstrating a cognitive cost for the increasing demands we require of ourselves. Stanford researchers found that multitasking reduces the efficiency and quality of our performance,[2] and the University of London conducted a study that found participants who multitasked experienced significant drops in IQ scores.[3] I think our obsession with breadth has diminished the depth of our interactions with our world, our work, and with each other. We want to do it all, even if we can't do it all well.

Are we missing the trees for the forest? Yes, I changed the words around on purpose. We are so lost in this forest of multitasking, that we don't even know how to look at a single tree anymore. Is the three-ring circus of life draining the joy from experiencing life the way God intended?

In Paul's letter to the *Colossians, 3:23,* he tells them, *"Whatever you do, work at it with all your heart, as working for the Lord, not for men."* All your heart, he says. Not a portion of my heart, or a fraction of my mind. *All my heart.* I would like to propose that single-tasking may be an act of worship.

Most of our time is spent either producing/performing or taking/absorbing. What if we were fully engaged in the moment of what we were doing? What if, as we prepared dinner, we marveled at the shapes, colors, and fragrance of the vegetables as we chopped the salad, instead of listening to the news or chatting through our speakerphone? What if we didn't try to distract ourselves with music or TV when we worked out, but we really focused on the response of our body as we exercise? What if we took a moment to quietly rest, and didn't turn on a single electronic device, but just absorbed the silence? What if we fully listened to the people who are talking to us – looking them in the eye and really processing everything they are saying?

God gave us five senses to experience the world he put us in, but our constant multitasking has dulled and devalued our senses. Jesus knew how to use his senses. When he looked at flowers, he saw truth. He told his disciples, *"Consider the lilies, how they grow: they neither toil nor spin, yet I tell you, even Solomon in all his glory was not arrayed like one of these."* Jesus seemed to find revelations about God everywhere, from the birds, to olive branches, and even mustard seeds. He harnessed God's power as he made mud to pat on the eyes of a blind man, and he heard stones ready to cry out the praises of God. His senses practiced the presence of God, and he was fully engaged in each moment.

I want to reawaken my senses, and fully focus on each thing I choose to do. I will not listen to my ego insist that the more things I do, the better I am. I will ignore the anxious lies that I don't have enough time to completely immerse myself in each task or pleasure. I will choose to do what I do with *all my heart.*

Brother Lawrence was a simple layman living in a French Monastery in the 1600's who practiced the presence of God in the lowly positions of kitchen service and sandal repair. His initial revelation of God's grace came from observing a barren tree in the winter and contemplating how the leafless branches waited patiently for the hope of spring. This spoke to him of God's unfailing grace and sovereignty.

Brother Lawrence continued to search for connections to God's love in simple and menial tasks. A man who no one should have ever heard of, became an inspiration to multitudes through his personal conversations and letters. Those letters became the classic Christian text, *The Practice of the Presence of God,*[4] and this book continues to inspire generations of believers. His 17th century gems of wisdom speak to my 21st century life: *"Never tire of doing even the smallest things for God, because he isn't impressed so much with the dimensions of our work, as with the love in which it is done."*

I start my single-tasking experiment on a weekend. I often over-plan my leisure time, and experience mental rope burn from the tug of war between what I should get done and what I really want to do. So the multitasking begins, and the chaos starts.

I actually stay very focused while I teach, though there are a multitude of demands on my teaching brain. Teachers are the most skilled of jugglers. We impart the knowledge, make the learning meaningful and keep the students engaged. In addition, we check for signs of understanding or confusion, maintain a defensive posture for behavioral interference, and adjust the pacing based on the student's needs, all while keeping an eye on the time. It's exhausting. Yet at the core of this flurry of activities is an objective. The educational objective – what we need to get the students to understand, to be able to do. All my mind juggling is focused on the purpose of my students achieving this learning objective. There exists that nucleus that drives all the subservient demands on my brain.

So maybe what I need this weekend are a few solid objectives. A realistic list of goals that will keep me focused. Goals not driven by compulsion, but rather pursued with intentionality. I will strive to single-task and attend to these goals with *all my heart.*

But I also know the importance of Sabbath. God told us to rest, to put aside work and enjoy the blessings and holiness of his creation. So I will make a realistic list that includes quiet time to really listen to music, not just to distract me from tasks. I will make time to smell, taste, and slowly enjoy a peppermint latte; Sit outside and feel the sun kiss my face; Sit under the night sky and watch for a shooting star.

One of my favorite childhood memories is laying on my tummy in the grass with my cousins looking for four-leaf clovers. We were not stalked by time, or distracted by obligations. We were lost in the microcosm forest of clovers, looking for that one unique specimen that represented a valuable treasure when found. That was when I truly knew how to single-task. Jesus told his disciples, *Unless you change and become like little children, you will never enter the kingdom of heaven. Matthew 18:3.* We often lose that sense of wonder in our hurried and cluttered lives.

It all seems idealistic when I talk or write about it: Do less, with a deeper focus and prioritize sensory experiences that seem like extravagances in a life where time reigns like a ruthless dictator.

But what I've learned about God's kingdom is that it is immune from the logic and boundaries of the world as we know it. People who have increased their giving or tithing in the midst of financial hardship can attest to this. God can do much with little and he reminds us that in his kingdom and economy: *My grace is sufficient for you, for my power is made perfect in weakness. - 2 Corinthians 12:9.*

So I write down my weekend goal list: Clean the garage, get the dog groomed, hand write some letters and birthday cards, and shop for groceries. I remind myself I want to do each task with *all my heart.* I intersperse my to-do list with times of stillness and worship. And I resolve that when I converse with anyone, I will cease my busyness, look in their eyes, and listen with *all my heart.*

By 10am I'm at the grocery store and I already feel the encroaching shadow of time begin to stalk me. I sigh when parking takes longer than it should and I feel my jaw tense when the line at the checkout moves slowly. I refocus on my way home and after putting away the groceries, I slip out to my patio for a Mary-moment at the feet of Jesus. *(Luke 10:38-42)*

This story in the gospels is one I've contemplated often. Jesus is at Martha's home and Martha's sister Mary is sitting at the feet of Jesus and absorbing everything he's saying. Martha is buzzing around in the kitchen with preparations. She complains to Jesus that Mary should be helping her. Jesus answers, *"Martha,*

Martha..." Whenever someone says your name twice, you can anticipate what's coming. He tells Martha that she is worried about many things, but few are needed, actually, only one. Then the gut punch. *"Mary has chosen what is better, and it will not be taken away from her."*

It takes a few minutes for me to quiet my soul, but soon I am absorbing the deep purple of the lavender blooms and thanking God for the palette of colors he blesses us with. But I feel like my Martha counterpart is watching me from the window – wondering when I will come inside and start the laundry. We all may have a little of both Mary and Martha in us, but Martha usually gets her way. It's hard to ignore her even though we know when we are with Jesus, we are right where we should be.

Brother Lawrence said he tried to live as if there were nothing in the world except Jesus and him. Easy for a childless bachelor living in a monastery you say. The ideals are indeed lofty, but I resolve not be heavy hearted when I fail. Life is a journey, and God already knows I am a slow learner. Baby steps are still steps.

Single-tasking requires discipline and practice. Brother Lawrence warned us not to get discouraged, because *"It takes a long while and a lot of hard work to develop this kind of habit."* Doing what I do with all my heart takes dedication and determination. Paul shared with the Philippians that he did not consider he had taken hold of his goals for Christ, yet he urged them to *Forget what is behind, and strain toward what is ahead. Philippians 3:13.*

When I reflect on the epic moments of my life, they are the times that are etched into my mind because absolutely nothing could compete for my focus. If I'm standing on the edge of the Grand Canyon, or watching the waves roll onto a beach, I don't feel the urge to do anything else but absorb the beauty. Yet I know there are smaller moments of beauty and holiness in each day that I miss because I am juggling too many tasks and looking in too many directions. I must be willing to look at the sky for a while to see a shooting star. I have to put my face to the ground to find a four-leaf clover.

I want to take back the gift of time that God blessed me with. I want to use all my senses to absorb every interaction. I want to spend each moment recognizing that he is right beside me, and attend to whatever I am doing as if I am doing it with him and for him, *with all my heart.*

Group discussion questions:

1. How often do you find yourself multitasking?

2. Do you feel it would be challenging to single-task more?

3. Do you think single-tasking can be an expression of worship?

4. How do you use your senses to engage with your life?

5. Think of a task you struggle with. What would it take to do it with all your heart?

6. How do you think you could implement these ideas?

Read and discuss these scripture passages:

Colossians 3:23-24

Psalms 19:1-4

Luke 10: 38-42

Philippians 3: 12-16

Time Bandits

For where your treasure is, there
your heart will be also.
Matthew 6:21

Billy Graham once said, give me five minutes with a person's checkbook, and I will tell you where their heart is. *If there's any Millennials or Generation Z's in your group, someone quickly explain to them what a checkbook is.*

How we spend our time reveals a lot about us as well. While Benjamin Franklin was the first that said "Time is Money," many of today's CEO's are agreeing that time is indeed the new currency. Netflix, General Electric, LinkedIn, and Virgin are among several companies who have implemented policy changes providing unlimited time off, citing it results in increased productivity via employee satisfaction and wellbeing. I even read about some companies that are offering employees paid sabbaticals to pursue their passions. Numerous surveys have revealed that many employees would prefer more time off in lieu of raises, and companies are listening.

Now obviously you won't see those survey results in a third world country. And even in our own cities, we have many people in poverty, who would gladly give up any amount of time to earn money to provide for their families and meet their basic needs. We also know there are those who sacrifice leisure time by working multiple jobs in order to just survive. For too many, free time is an unrelatable luxury, and may even be an uncomfortable reminder of their own limited resources.

I think it's our human condition to *want* for something. If our basic needs are met, we always find more we think we need or want. If we achieve some financial stability, we naturally want more time to enjoy the fruits of our hard work. Yet we never seem to have enough of it.

Let's look back a generation or two. When my Dad was a boy, he did his chores and homework, played baseball in the park, and after dinner, the family sat around the radio listening to news, music, or drama. Seems like a simpler, slower pace of life.

Compare that with what competes for our attention now. Sometimes I imagine traveling back in time to when my parents bought their first black and white television with three channels. I remember watching the Beatles sing on the Ed Sullivan show on that tiny box when I was five years old. My mom and grandma couldn't understand all the fuss over them.

I try to imagine my parent's reaction if I told them in the future people would have multiple *color* TVs in their homes, cars, and even on their refrigerators. And how the channels and choices would be too numerous to count. Can you see their faces drop in shock? Add in video games and music systems, internet, phones, and all the other technology and entertainment devices we demand. A lot has changed in just a single generation.

What else do we do with our leisure time? We go out to eat and enjoy various forms of entertainment, such as movies, sports, and concerts. We work out at the gym, and cram in those appointments for dentists, oil changes, or the salon. Then there are the kids. We feel obligated to pull them away from the magnetism of video games, so we sign them up for sports, gymnastics, drama, or karate. None of these things are bad, it's just that the excessive amount of options we have reflects on, well,…*our excess.* Somehow we have bought into the thinking that *success means full and busy.* The busier we are, the more important we are, and the happier we must be. Some sociologists believe that busyness has become a type of status symbol. I'm reminded of a quote from Corrie ten Boom, *"If the devil cannot make us bad, he will make us busy.*"

I'm guessing the objections are already forming in your mind. *But I work hard, I deserve a game of golf on the weekend; Yoga helps me relax and keeps me healthy;* Fill in your own blank here. Maybe some of you are thinking, *What leisure time? My kids take up all my time; My job doesn't stop on the weekends.* When it comes to how we spend our time or money, we are all quick to judge others, but exceptional at rationalizing our own choices.

I anticipate that many will feel their job demands more of their time than they are comfortable with. It's a difficult area, because we often feel we can't risk losing our jobs by objecting to the obligations that are required of us. If you have a boss that asks for an unreasonable amount of your time, anonymously gift him or her this book with this page bookmarked, and this sentence highlighted. Then pray.

It is easy to succumb to the belief that we have little control over how our time is spent. We've heard the stats before that we spend one-third of our life sleeping, five years waiting in lines, six years in the bathroom, two years returning phone calls, and the list goes on. That's life, we say. We can't control it.

Now here is where it gets personal. Time management can be like looking in a mirror under fluorescent lights. I'd rather stay in the warm and flattering candlelight, but if I really want to see the flaws, I need to be brave enough to face the magnified mirror. Like most self-improvement, it takes some brave and honest self-reflection, goal setting, and determination. Only you can make these decisions and determine the value to how you spend your time.

Most blueprints for battle plans consist of the following steps:
1. Understand the problem or opponent
2. Develop your best strategy
3. Fight the battle with all you have

Prayerful reflection is always the best place to start. I encourage you to take an inventory of how you spend your time each day. Find an hourly planner grid that will work for you. There are several online you can customize. For a week, record your activities, as accurately as you can. You might be thinking you already know what this exercise will show. I am hoping you will be willing to participate, as I am sure you will make some discoveries.

Remember this is a SELF-reflection. It is for you only, so please be honest, and don't try to stack the deck to impress anyone. The point is for you to assess how you spend your time, and set personal goals based on what you discover. Ask the Holy Spirit to reveal his wisdom and will for you.

After you have identified some of the time bandits in your life, decide on a strategy to overcome them. Baby steps are good. Goals are best mastered when they are achievable. Resolve to:

1. Pray for support and wisdom
2. Try your best
3. Beware of guilt or pride (don't compare yourself to others)
4. Have no judgement (for yourself or others)
5. Learn from the experience

Remember behavioral experts tell us that it takes at least twenty-one days to create a new habit, but it takes approximately ninety days to break an old habit. Change is hard. Just whisper, *I can do all things through Christ who strengthens me. Philippians 4:13*

We all learn and grow in different ways. I urge you to celebrate all growth, no matter how small. Remember the goal is taking back the GIFT of time. Remind yourself often that time is a gift from God. You are just trying to become a better steward of this gift.

I expect that every person who takes this challenge will have a different experience. I can't or won't begin to predict what the Holy Spirit will reveal to you through this exercise. It's not about any activity being good or bad. It is about reflecting and prioritizing, and letting the Holy Spirit do some reorganizing in our life. After all, He wants us to live life abundantly. *(John 10:10)*

Let's reflect on the word *priority*. I just used it as a verb, and now I'm reading how the plural form of this word, *priorities*, didn't even exist until around the 1940's. The Oxford Dictionary defines priority: *The fact or condition of being regarded or treated as more important than others.* For centuries, *priority* meant one thing that was valued more than anything else. One thing. Making it plural diminishes it.

So what is your one priority? Does this question feel like one of those exercises where you have to choose who from the sinking ship gets to go into the lifeboat? What if *our priority* was actually the lifeboat himself?

As Christians, the pat answer is: our priority is our Creator and Savior. We believe it, but our lives don't often reflect it. Often the more secure something is to us, the less urgency we feel toward it. When I know something will be there, I feel I can put it off until later. The Cambridge dictionary defines: *Take something for granted*, this way: To never think about something because you believe it will always be available or stay exactly the same.

I admit, my time with the Lord sometimes falls into this reasoning. I know God is always there for me, so surely he won't mind if I do these urgent tasks with deadlines first. I will be more focused if I just get this task behind me. I am a master at justifying my rationale. Yet I know that he longs to be my true (singular) priority.

In the story where Jesus feeds the five thousand. *(John 6)* The disciple Andrew says to Jesus, *"Here is a boy with five small barley loaves and two small fish, but how far will they go among so many?"* Isn't that how we feel sometimes when we look at our to-do list? There's a limited number of minutes in each day, how can I accomplish all I need to do? But Jesus answered, *"Have the people sit down."* Then he took the loaves and fish and gave thanks. And everyone had *enough.* Maybe if we just sit down with Jesus, and thank him, there will be enough minutes too. Maybe more than enough.

I'm writing this study for myself. I know how I spend my time does not often reflect my priority. I know much of my time is spent selfishly, and much is wasted, even during my most efficient days. I believe God is calling me to honor the gift of time he has given me.

In the next chapter, I bare my soul to give you the courage to reflect on your own time bandits. His word encourages me to confess my struggles, *(James 5:16)* and promises me that his grace is sufficient, and his power is made perfect in my weakness. *(2 Corinthians 12:9)*

Group discussion questions:

1. How do you feel when you are facing an especially busy day or demanding week? How do you deal with it?

2. Do you think we view busyness as fulfillment? Is busyness a status symbol?

3. Are you willing to record your life activities for a week so you can evaluate how you spend your time?

4. Do you think you may identify some time bandits in your life?

5. Do you think how you spend your time reflects your priorities?

Read and discuss these scripture passages:

John 6: 1-13

2 Corinthians 9:6-15

Matthew 6:33-34

Surviving Without Survivor

Do not be conformed to this world,
but be transformed by the renewal of
your mind, that by testing you may
discern what is the will of God, what
is good and acceptable and perfect.
Romans 12:2

Before I started my time inventory, I knew one thing it would reveal: I watch too much television. I indulged in thirty-two seasons of *Survivor* before I came to my senses and extinguished the torch of mindlessness. Sanity has spoken, and that tribe is now mute. The thought of how many hours I spent watching people sabotage each other for fortune is embarrassing.

I watch movies, documentaries, history and science shows, and I love nature shows like Blue Planet. There's junk food in my television diet as well, but I can proudly say I've never watched anything with the word *housewives* in the title.

I'm very good at justifying my indulgence. I rationalize that through T.V. I stay educated on current events and issues, and increase my knowledge of many topics. As the yet undiscovered writer of several story scripts, I love to immerse myself in drama plots and story structures that help me analyze and improve my writing.

There's truth in all of these persuasions, as well as the simple fact that when I get home from a long day at work, cook dinner, and attend to all that life requires, I'm just too tired to do anything but surrender my mind as a spectator to someone else's story – real or imaginary. But the bottom line is that watching T.V. steals time from my life. How do I resolve to take this time back? This is a hard one for me.

I've been on several fasts with my church, and I have found it easier for me to give up food than the internet or television. Stories, words, and ideas have a stronger hold on my brain than sugar, fat, or carbs have on my body. We all have our little addictions in life.

You may think the word addiction is too strong, and I don't in any way compare this with substance abuse addictions. My heart hurts for people who are in that extremely difficult battle. Psychologists describe addiction as a condition that results when a person consumes a substance or engages in an activity that can be pleasurable, but the continuation of which becomes compulsive or interferes with ordinary responsibilities and relationships.

In 2015, the Collins English Dictionary chose the word *binge-watch* as the word of the year. This word emerged to describe the marathon television viewing that resulted when Netflix began releasing entire seasons of serial programs. Whether or not binge-watching is an addiction, it is absolutely a powerful time bandit.

I know some of the activities that steal time in my life may interfere with my relationship with Jesus, who is *My Priority.* One thing I have learned is: If you ask God to grow you and pray that he will align your will with his, and if you honestly desire to *break free from the patterns of this world and be transformed by the renewing of your mind,* you can expect some changes in your life.

I've found that most of what diverts us away from Jesus, and away from true freedom, often falls into the areas of *control* or *escapism.* Control is an active response, while escapism is passive.

When we lean into *escapism*, we distract ourselves from our realities by immersing ourselves in an alternative reality. Escapism can be relatively harmless, involving art, music, books, or sports; or life altering, such as with alcohol, drugs, or sexual perversions.

My watching T.V. can be called entertainment, but it's also a little bit of escapism. While I'm watching that movie, I'm not thinking about the cost of reroofing my house or my best friend's health struggles. The story takes my brain on a detour and it is happy to get away for a while. This is most likely why the entertainment industry was booming during the Great Depression. Musicals, comedies, gangster films, and radio shows distracted Americans from their everyday struggles.

Great works of literature deserve to be celebrated, and we should appreciate the creativity of those who have used entertainment to stretch our imagination, take us to places we might never see, or open our minds to respect and empathize with those who are different than us. But we can't deny our significant attraction to this escapism when we tabulate the billions of dollars spent on movies and television every year.

On the flip side, when we lean into *controlling* something, we feel empowered. It cloaks our own vulnerability, at least temporarily. This is why we often have reactive responses to unsettling circumstances. We take the offense to diverge ourselves from feelings and fears that make us uncomfortable. Sometimes control can take a huge toll on our relationships.

We also see our tendencies to control when we micromanage, exhibit compulsive behaviors, or excessively cling to rules and routines. We naturally don't like unpredictability or disorder, so we seek for ways to establish dominion and control when we can.

A few years ago, our church was doing its yearly January fasting time, and I decided along with a once a week food fast, I would refrain from purchasing anything for myself. After the month was over, I felt inclined to continue in abeyance for the entire year. I still shopped for groceries and hygiene items, but I purchased no clothes, shoes, jewelry, personal items, or indulgences for myself.

I knew that God was teaching me something. Shopping made me feel in control. When I made a purchase, I felt happy, like I had rewarded myself. I think this is why some women joke about "shopping therapy." In our lives, we have to deal with many things that are beyond our control, and we subconsciously search for experiences we *can* control. I can walk into a mall, and come out with a new pair of shoes, simply because I decided to. Buying something usually makes us feel good, although it's only temporary, but it sometimes results in buyer's remorse later.

Through that year of no purchases, I came to experience a freedom over the false feeling of control that shopping tempted me with. I was not trying to be pious, and only my family knew of my commitment. I simply wanted to renew my mind and break free from this artificial gratification.

Sometimes our insecurity or vanity may steal our time. Do we spend too much time trying to look and feel beautiful by the world's standards? Or maybe we obsess with wanting our houses to look like the examples in the home makeover shows.

I'm not suggesting anyone give up shopping or television or makeup. I'm only transparently sharing my experiences with you to encourage you to do your own reflection. Observe how you spend your time and ask the Holy Spirit to provide wisdom to you. Growth almost always requires letting go of something. When we surrender something we have been holding onto, we are free to take hold of new gifts from him.

We have a tangible reminder for this spiritual concept. He gave us two hands to work with, eat with, and love with. With our hands we hold onto things, or release them. We make choices about what we hold onto physically, mentally, and spiritually. Look at your hands. Open them and close them. Grab hold of something, then put it down and pick up something new. Wasn't that easy? Holding and letting go, giving and receiving, is all about choices, and our free will to make those choices. Are you holding tightly onto anything that is stealing your time?

This reflection is not intended to condemn any activity. Maybe you spend your time doing what you do because you are passionate about it and you fully enjoy it. That is wonderful! I just think it's good to ask ourselves why we cling to the things we do. Could it be giving us a sense of control? Is it distracting us from some of the stress we feel? We have the freedom to choose how we spend our time, but God wants us to experience true freedom in the choices we make.

I'm guessing you picked up this book for a reason. I've been praying it would reach people who are sharing my struggles with time management, and initiate a dialogue that would lift us all to a higher place. So now is the time for me to ask you: *If you wrote this chapter, what would your title be?* Don't answer right away. Let the question hover in your mind over the next few days. Pray and listen for Holy Spirit wisdom.

Are you willing to give up something that steals your time for maybe just one day? Many people would struggle to refrain from social media for even a single day. But stepping away from the time bandits in our life is a step away from external influences, and a step toward regaining the gift of time.

I am not yet where I want to be, and I may never arrive. I still watch too much television, and spend too little time with Jesus. I still get stressed with my to-do lists, and find myself wasting time with trivial time bandits. But I am pushing forward for the renewing of my mind. I have accepted that *there is no "there", there.* My love for my Creator drives me to seek the freedom and purpose he has for me. Near the end of his life, Paul said, *"I have fought the good fight, I have finished the race."* *(2 Tim 4:7)* I may never feel like I have finished the race, but I want to keep running forward until I draw my last breath.

Group discussion questions:

1. Do you see possibilities of control or escapism in your life?

2. Is there a time you have let go of something that had a hold of you? What were the results?

3. What do you see interfering with your priorities?

4. Are you willing to surrender one of these time bandits for a day? A week? Longer?

5. Would you be willing to share your experience, successes and struggles, with your group?

Read and discuss these scripture passages:
1 Corinthians 10:23
Philippians 3:13-14
Romans 12:2
1 John 2:15-17
Matthew 6:19-34

Stop and Smell the Roses

Be still and know that I am God.
Psalms 46:10

Every time I read or hear this scripture, it has a profound effect on me. *Be still.* My soul seems to stop in its tracks. Oh, how he knows me. *Know that I am God.* I know he is God, but he wants me to *Be still* and *know.*

Earlier we contemplated some of the repercussions of multitasking. I think this merits revisiting, because it has become so ingrained into the way we do life, that it now takes much discipline for us to simply do one thing at a time.

Researchers have determined that this rapid task juggling which we like to call multitasking, uses up oxygenated glucose in our brains, which actually deteriorates our focus. To combat these physiological effects, we tend to reach for a quick fix of sugar, carbs, or caffeine. What our brain really needs is to stop and take a break. And not a break to check Facebook, email, or our phone, but to actually let your mind rest and wander, without dictating what it needs to be doing.

The word multitasking didn't even really exist until the 1960's. It came about as a description for the capabilities of computers. So I guess we decided that if computers can do it, we should be able to also. Everywhere we go, we see the chaos of the world feeding into our appetite for multitasking. Restaurants and bars have dozens of TVs with multiple channels playing at once. Even as I work on this chapter, I'm toggling between five open windows on my computer to aid in my research and word choice.

After I wrote chapter five, I started seeing more and more research and evidence that we were not designed to be multitaskers. In fact, what I began to notice, is that there is actually an inherent design for rest and reflection woven into the rhythms of our lives.

As a reading teacher, I sometimes read research on how the brain handles reading tasks. When we read, our eyes move across strings of words quickly, and then rest briefly on select words. The sweeps over word strings are called saccades, and the landing points are called fixations. These stops within eye movements are so extremely fast and automatic, we are unaware of them happening.

By studying readers using sophisticated eye tracking devices, researchers are able to better understand the cognitive processing that happens, as well as determine how struggling readers process words compared with efficient readers. I'll spare you too much detail, but the point I want to highlight is that researchers have determined that information is only uploaded to our brain during the fixations. The eyes have to stop moving for the brain to understand what the eyes are taking in.

I also stumbled onto an article in a nutritional magazine that explained how food can only digest when we stop eating. It seems we are designed to "be still" for our brains and body to function properly. I began to think more about how multitasking interferes with our ability to properly absorb and reflect. When we juggle from task to task, we leave no room for this contemplation, no room for closure.

In the first chapter of Genesis, after each day's creation, we are told *God saw that it was good.* He paused and reflected on what he had made. The creation story unfolds with a sense of divine order and perfect focus. The intentionality reveals to us that everything God creates has his entire focus. *And it is good.*

Take a deep breath. Breathe in and out. Something we were not taught, yet we do every day of our life. We rarely think about it, yet every function of our existence depends upon those breaths. Someone encouraged me once to whisper prayerful words with each inhale and exhale when I need to reset.

Call to the Lord with the inhale. Breathe in as you say: *Jesus,* or *Father,* or *Yahweh*, or your favorite term of endearment for our Lord, and then a statement of faith as you exhale. I chose: *"Abba,"* for the inhale and *"I belong to you."* For the exhale.

Perhaps you've seen the word *Selah* in the Psalms or Book of Habakkuk. Bible scholars have differing theories as to why this word is frequently used. Many think it means *pause,* or *think hard about this.* When you read *Selah*, stop and let the preceding words upload to your brain and download to your heart.

> *In your anger do not sin; When you*
> *are on your beds, search your hearts*
> *and be silent. Selah. (Psalms 4:4)*

> *Who is he, this king of glory? The*
> *Lord Almighty – he is the king of*
> *glory. Selah. (Psalms 24:10)*

> *You are my hiding place; you will*
> *protect me from trouble and*
> *surround me with songs of*
> *deliverance. Selah. (Psalms 32:7)*

I need to write Selah after every scripture I read. In fact, I think I need *Selah* embedded into everything I do. Even when I consciously refrain from multitasking, my mind drifts off to what is next on my agenda. Do you know anyone you would like to hide the remote control from because they just can't seem to stop surfing through the television channels? Well sometimes I feel like I need to hide the remote that controls my wandering brain.

Why is living in the moment so hard for us? We have conditioned ourselves to pursue everything in a linear way, and the unachievable finish line pulls us like gravity away from the present moment. What are we missing? I sometimes think my lack of "Selahs" or reflection times are keeping me from uploading the truths and absorbing the joys that God intends for me. Like a tree that thrives from deep watering, frequent surface sprinkles will not result in the strong, deep roots required for healthy growth and stability. In our lives, we often choose to go fast and wide over going deep.

Frank Laubach was a missionary in the Philippines in the early 1900's. While working among Muslims there, he was distressed with the devastating poverty of the people, and developed a literacy program that has helped millions of people learn to read in their own language. Dr. Laubach spent a lifetime bringing his vision and approach for achieving literacy to over one hundred countries around the world. He also wrote over forty books on literacy, prayer, and justice, and he traveled the world, inspiring many with his vision for literacy and peace.

Kind of a busy guy. His life makes my daily agenda look like a lazy siesta. Yet this amazing man is also known for his lofty goal of an unceasing focus on God and prayer. His passion unfolds in his letters published in the book, *Letters by a Modern Mystic,*[5] and he is best known for his book called *The Game with Minutes,*[6] written in 1953.

In this book, Christians are challenged to keep God in their mind for at least one second of every waking minute. The idea of tuning into God once each minute seems unimaginable, but I think I may actually know some people who do the *Game with Minutes* with their phones. The book guides believers in how to bring God into one's mind as they proceed through daily life. Laubach stated, *"We shall not become like Christ until we give him more time."* Laubach practiced this presence of God and documented his experiences:

> *"All during the day, in the chinks of time between the things we find*

ourselves obliged to do, there are the moments when our minds ask: 'What next?' In these chinks of time, ask Him: 'Lord, think Thy thoughts in my mind. What is on Thy mind for me to do now?' When we ask Christ, 'What next?' we tune in and give Him a chance to pour His ideas through our enkindled imagination. If we persist, it becomes a habit."

One of the revelations in Laubach's teachings is the emphasis on listening to God. Too often we fill our prayer time with many words and requests, neglecting the time to listen for what God might want to say to us. Conversation is a two-way street. Have you ever known someone who loves to talk but doesn't listen well? Is this how we pray? Listening takes practice. Don't hear anything? Wait. Listen harder.

The Holy Spirit of God speaks to us in many different ways. Sometimes he brings someone to my mind, and I pray for them or call them. Sometimes he brings a scripture to my mind that encourages me in an area I am struggling in. There are a few times he has brought a visual image to my mind that has spoken to me in ways that words cannot. And sometimes, things happen that reveal his Father's heart for us in a way that is unique and specific to only us. I call these *God Kisses*.

My friend Joanne hears from God through her dreams. With my friend Chris, a song will often come to her mind that speaks to her. My friend Trish often shares a devotional that has spoken to her heart. Is there a time when God has revealed himself to you through his amazing and beautiful creation? Our Lord is not limited to words. The creator of creativity has many unique ways to speak to us. He will speak, but we must *be still* to listen.

But what about when God seems to be silent? A few years ago

I read a book about Mother Theresa, *Come Be My Light.*[7] This collection of her private letters reveal her heartache with experiencing a long silence from God, even as she served him with full abandon. She had very clearly heard God call her to her unique mission field in 1946, then spent most of her life longing to hear from him again in the same intimate way.

This sense of abandonment, often referred to as *The Dark Night of the Soul*, has been experienced and described by many mystics throughout history, including 16th century Saint John of the Cross, and 19th century Saint Therese. Though hard to understand why some of the most devout Christians have walked through this dark night of faith, it's purpose seems to be a deep trust that perhaps can grow no other way.

Reading Mother Theresa's soul-bearing letters in this book made me admire her all the more. What a faith it takes to love and serve God when he seems silent. Mother Theresa's boundless ability to love and understand the suffering of the poor thrived within her own loneliness and suffering. A woman that had no attachments to anything material or any comforts of the world, could only experience suffering through the silence of God in her life.

I am guessing most people who have had a long relationship with God have experienced some silent times as I have. Any long term relationship is prone to ebbs and flows. I have always loved the raw honesty of the Psalms. David, whom God called "A man after my own heart," was candid about his struggles:

> *How long, Lord? Will you forget me*
> *forever? How long will you hide*
> *your face from me? How long must I*
> *wrestle with my thoughts and day*
> *after day have sorrow in my heart?*
> *Psalms 13: 1,2*

Yet David still calls out to God in prayer, and proclaims:
> *But I will trust in your unfailing love; My heart rejoices in your salvation. (verse 5).*

If you experience silent times from God, you are in the good company of King David, Mother Theresa, and many others. Yet they followed him and trusted him even in the silence.

Think back to a time when you were first falling in love with someone. In the beginning, you want to know everything about them. You can't ask enough questions. You share stories, thoughts and dreams. As your relationship grows over time, you reach a point where you can just be together, in silence, and bask in the closeness and love of that person. I think intimacy with God can be the same way.

I've been married to my husband for over thirty years. He knows more about me than anyone, and we have weathered the good and bad and unexpected that life throws at you. We have been angry with each other, yet loved deeply and unconditionally.

Likewise, my relationship with God has had peaks and valleys. I know I will love him, and be loved by him, whatever life brings. There have been times I have been angry or neglectful, but I am in this relationship for the long run. He is part of my life whether I ignore him or commune with him. But in my heart, I know I was created for this relationship.

From Brother Lawrence to Frank Laubach, and many other writers and prophets throughout time, we have been encouraged and challenged to practice the presence of God in our daily life. No one has suggested that this is an easy achievement, but one that takes conscious discipline. Sometimes we need to remove ourselves from the noise and chaos of our life to be able to hear from God. Even Jesus pulled himself away from the people and distractions, and retreated often in solitude to be with his Father.

When Mary sat at the feet of Jesus, all she wanted was to hear from him. Martha had a harder time with the *Be still* part. And Jesus said, *"Mary has chosen what is better...."*

We have choices too. I have a little graphic by my computer workspace. It says: God gave you a gift of 86,400 seconds today. Have you used one to say "Thank you"? Use just a few of those seconds right now and take a deep breath in and say his name. Exhale and wait. Listen. *Be still* and *know* him.

Group discussion questions:

1. Do you think you would benefit from more reflection time? Where do you think Selah moments might fit into your life?

2. What do you think about Frank Laubach's challenge to connect with God once every minute? Do you think it's attainable?

3. Share a time when you feel you have heard from God. Was it through his words, a dream, his creation, or something else?

4. How could you "Be Still," in order to have more reflection time or connections with God in your day?

Read and discuss these scripture passages:

Matthew 6:6-8

Luke 5:16, Luke 6:12, Mark 1:35, Mark 6:46

Matthew 14:23

Romans 8: 26-27

Carpe Diem

Jesus said, "No procrastination. No
backward looks. You can't put God's
kingdom off till tomorrow. Seize the
day."   Luke 9:62 (Message Bible)

I think the Message version of this verse may be the only one that adds *Seize the day*, but it seems very appropriate to what Jesus is saying to us here. *Carpe Diem* originally came from the Roman Poet, Horace in 23 B.C., but was ushered into contemporary usage in a speech made by actor Robin Williams in the 1989 film, *Dead Poets Society*.[8] Since then, we have heard this call to embrace each moment of our life in countless speeches and songs.

How do we seize the day rather than letting the days seize us? We have so many *if* and *when* excuses. *If* I was younger, *if* I was wealthier, *if* I wasn't so busy...*When* my kids are grown, *when* I retire, *when I have more time...*

As long as we see time as linear, we can push our goals into the peripheral vision of our fuzzy future. I think the answer lies in comprehending time as the gift that it is. Each moment is a present to be opened and cherished.

I imagine opening a present from God, and inside is a beautiful bottle filled with "time." Would I put this precious gift on a shelf to just look at? Save it for the future? Hide it so no one steals it? Dump it down the drain because the expiration date has passed? Or should I enjoy it to the fullest, generously share it, and savor every sip?

The Greek language has two words for time: *Chronos* and *Kairos*. Chronos is where we get our word *chronological*. Chronos is time that can be measured with clocks and calendars. It is predictable and constant in our life. I set an alarm clock to wake me up at 5:30, and I program my phone to remind me to pay bills on the 15th of the month. I know today the sun will set at 7:41 P.M., and I have three more years until I retire.

Kairos time is harder to define and understand. It is a season or moment of time, a window of opportunity, a sacred appointment. Chronos is quantitative, where kairos is qualitative.

Both Greek words kairos and chronos are found in the original language of the Bible. Kairos is used over eighty times in the New Testament. The word kairos is used when Jesus said....*My time has not yet come, (John 7:6-8)* and when speaking about the end of days, *(Mark 13:26, 32-33)*. Kairos moments seem to have a sovereign distinction. Actually it seems the Bible is full of people who seized significant kairos moments. Reflect on the stories of Abraham, Moses, David, Daniel, Paul, or pick your favorite Bible hero or heroine, and think about the kairos moments that landed them on the chronos timeline.

I don't think I'll ever be called to lead a nation out of slavery, or slay a giant, or interpret a king's dream, but I'm pretty sure I've had my own kairos moments. I think a kairos moment can simply be when we step out of the boundaries of a chronos mindset.

Peter, Andrew, James, and John had an opportunity to seize the day when Jesus asked them to follow him. They dropped their nets and left their boats immediately. And their lives were never the same. Kairos moments are often great catalysts for change.

I've heard so many stories of people who have experienced what is often referred to as a *divine appointment*. These are encounters when it seems the timing was perfect for your path to intersect with someone who God wanted you to meet or talk to, or maybe you've experienced an inconvenient delay or detour that later revealed a significant outcome. When God's timing (and will) aligns with our timing (and will), supernatural portals open.

I've experienced some of my own kairos moments, but I know I've missed a few too. I've ignored the promptings of the Holy Spirit, because I felt too busy. I'm ready to stop feeling threatened by time and instead receive time as the gift that it is. I believe if I seize the kairos moments in any given day, I can't possibly feel that my day was a failure.

I'm asking God to open my eyes and heart to see and hear the opportunities he places before me each day. How sweet as I lay my head down at night, to reflect on the moments of my day when time didn't matter, rather than dwell on the unfinished tasks and the pressing demands of tomorrow.

Sometimes I think about the defining moments of my life. Those times when God gave me such a gift, the impact sculpted my life and formed my identity. I clearly remember my third grade teacher complimenting my writing skills, though it was a very long time ago. I do not know the date, the day, and I would have to think for a bit to even tell you what year it was. This moment of time is vague on the chronological timeline of my life, but it is etched permanently as the kairos moment when I first began to see myself as a writer.

In my teen years I remember seeing Corrie ten Boom speak at a youth camp I attended. Corrie and her family helped hide Jews from the Gestapo during World War II. The ten Boom family saved many people before they were caught and sent to concentration camps. Corrie's unfathomable stories of her time in captivity at Ravensbrück with her sister Betsie, planted seeds of compassion in me for those who keep faith through suffering and oppression.

Corrie lost her father, and eventually her dearly loved sister, yet her triumphing faith in the darkest of situations has been an inspiration for my own faith walk time and again. Corrie was finally released, due to a simple clerical error that miraculously spared her from the gas chamber. This little woman of great faith was later able to forgive two of her captors in person.

After hearing her speak, I read her books, and have thought of her often as the seeds of mercy, empathy, faith, and forgiveness, have grown deep in my heart. These seeds have grown and led to my own experiences and relationships with immigrants and the homeless. That night, over forty years ago, when I sat and listened to Corrie speak, was a kairos moment for me.

What are your kairos moments? Think back and think hard. These moments, truly gifts from God, have shaped who you are and led you to places and people that have impacted you in many ways. Reflect on your kairos moments, and offer thanks to God for them. Then look forward to even more kairos moments to come. They are another example of the gift of time.

I am thankful for the people God has put in my path who were willing to give of their time to impact and inspire me. If I made a list of the moments that are imprinted in my heart and mind, I would only be able to tell you the chronos time for a few of them.

The days my son and daughter were born are certainly kairos moments, because my life and perspective changed profoundly when they were born. I will never forget these chronological dates because we celebrate their birthdays every year.

However, I do not know the chronological date when I sat on the floor at the feet of Rev. Martin Luther King, Sr. listening to him speak about his son's fight for justice. And I can't tell you which Sunday I read the memo in the church bulletin asking for people to go on a mission trip to Belize. These were moments that became life sculpting opportunities for me. My ears and heart were open to receive something that would impact my life, and possibly other's lives through me.

I encourage you to reflect on your life and identify some of the kairos moments that have impacted you. They are there, woven into the fabric of what makes you who you are. Sometimes our defining moments may even be ones of pain, but I believe God is true to his word that he works everything together for good to those who love him. *(Romans 8:28)* Even in my pain, mistakes, failures, and detours, he has found a way to grow me, and redeem my heartaches for a stronger faith. Where we ourselves have suffered, this is where we are most able to empathize and minister to others.

In kairos moments, we may be the receiver, or the giver. If we stop looking at the clock, and instead pay attention to the faces of the people we cross paths with, we might just become the source of a kairos moment for someone else.

Contemplating kairos moments helps me to step out of the chaos of the chronos mindset. I search for these moments every day. Lord, help me to see these opportunities to step out of the blur of each day and seize the gems that you are setting before me. As the Psalmist sings in Psalms 84: *Better is one day in your courts, than a thousand elsewhere.*

Group discussion questions:

1. What "if and when" excuses keep you from seizing the day?

2. Think about one of your favorite Bible heroes or heroines. What were some of their Kairos moments?

3. Can you remember any defining moments in your past? How did these times shape who you are today?

4. Can you share a time you experienced a Kairos moment? Were you the receiver or the giver of the moment?

Read and discuss these scripture passages:

Matthew 4:18-22

Luke 9:57-62

Ephesians 5:15-16

Philippians 3:13-14

Isaiah 43:18-19

Molasses in January

The Lord is not slow in keeping his
promise, as some understand
slowness. Instead, he is patient with
you, not wanting anyone to perish,
but everyone to come to repentance.
2 Peter 3:9

In the Civil War epic, *Gone With the Wind,*[9] Scarlett O'Hara scolds the young slave Prissy for being "Slow as Molasses in January." This expression is thought to have originated in the late 1800's, and was used to describe everything from horse-drawn street cars to the workings of Congress. However, in January of 1919, this idiom lost its jovial charm when 2.5 million gallons of molasses burst out of a large storage tank, flooding the streets of Boston.

This is what happens when I am lured into the jungle of the internet. My husband swears that molasses helps his joints feel better. Skeptical, I enlisted Google to research his claim. One click led to another and soon I stumbled onto this bizarre molasses disaster story. This great molasses flood actually knocked over buildings and vehicles, and even killed horses and people. Now if only I played trivial pursuit or Jeopardy, I might be able to justify the time I've just spent reading about this. Maybe I'll file it away for my next movie script idea.

How quickly I can digress. The analogies of dripping molasses or watching grass grow are all too accurate when we are waiting for something that is important to us. Science explains why time is not absolute, but the real paradox for me is how it can seem to be going too fast and too slow at the same time. It all depends on what we are measuring with the passage of time.

When we are waiting for something we desperately desire, time can seem like an agent of torture. The watched pot stubbornly refuses to boil.

When we pray for people we love who are hurting, or suffering, or in need of Jesus, our wait can seem painfully long. When we struggle with our health, or finances, or broken relationships, days can seem like weeks, weeks like months, and months like years. When we work towards difficult goals, or wait for our big dreams, time mimics a slow motion sloth on a transcontinental journey.

I have some big dreams with precarious odds. I've written three movie scripts that I would love to see on the big screen someday. Six years ago, when praying for a way to make a difference for the homeless, I read Martin Luther's quote: *"If you want to change the world, pick up your pen and write."* Realizing how stories can change people's hearts, I began to write stories that would put human faces on the issues I cared deeply about.

As a teacher in Phoenix who doesn't have contacts in Hollywood, my only option with my finished scripts was to enter them in contests. Over the last five years, I've scored high enough to keep me encouraged and working on rewrites. But I have to be honest, my heart still sinks in heaviness with every rejection letter. I believe that the Creator of creativity has blessed me with ideas, ability, and perseverance, and there must be a destination for these stories that I've poured my heart into. My faith wavers at times, but I am also aware that with each rejection, I have accomplished rewrites that have made my stories better.

My big dreams might sound foolish, or trivial compared to what you are praying for. I have friends who are praying for loved ones who struggle with addictions or terminal illnesses. I know others who are praying to get a job and get off the street and into a home. We all sometimes wonder why our prayers take so long to get answered.

There is a lot of waiting in the Bible. The prophet Habakkuk was waiting for God to answer his pleas for help and he questioned God's inaction.

We can hear the desperation in the first chapter of Habakkuk:

> *"How long, O Lord, must I call for*
> *help, but you do not listen? Or cry*
> *out to you 'violence!' but you do not*
> *save?"*

Abraham and Sarah, Moses, Joseph, Daniel, and many others in the Bible experienced extended times of waiting for God to deliver. Yet the waiting period is where the real story happens.

In the waiting, we see the character of these men and women, and we see the sovereignty of God. Abraham and Sarah grew tired of waiting and took the matter of securing God's promise of descendants into their own hands. Yet they still lived to see God deliver his promise in *his* timing. *(Genesis 15, 16)* The message of each story is clear – Trust God through the waiting.

The bookend to Habakkuk's lament is one of my favorites:

> *"Though the fig tree does not bud*
> *and there are no grapes on the vines,*
> *though the olive crop fails and the*
> *fields produce no food, though there*
> *are no sheep in the pen and no cattle*
> *in the stalls, yet I will rejoice in the*
> *Lord, I will be joyful in God my*
> *Savior".*

I think there is an orchestrated purpose to God's timing, and often it means we have to wait. God has set us in a world with seasons and cycles of planting, waiting, and harvesting. His design is woven into all of creation.

In Psalms 19, David proclaims:

The heavens declare the glory of God; the skies proclaim the work of his hands. Day after day they pour forth speech; night after night they display knowledge.

Sometimes I think all of God's creation speaks to us, if we will listen. There are reminders everywhere that beauty often comes with great price. My Mexican bird of Paradise plant blooms like crazy after I have given it a brutal pruning. This reminds me that sometimes we require pruning because God knows what it takes to create new growth and make us bloom.

Gold is purified at 1000 degrees, and diamonds almost as old as the earth were formed under conditions of intense heat and extreme pressure. Even a beautiful pearl is formed by an irritant inside the body of an oyster. All around us, we see beauty that took upheaval, pressure, refinement, and time. Lots of time. If it seems like God is not in a hurry, remember he is more concerned about the perfect and beautiful outcome.

I threaded some beads on a *chenille stem*. When I was a kid we called these pipe cleaners, but I guess that's old school. Now they are "chenille stems." *Did you know chenille is French for caterpillar?* Yikes, there I go again!

The beads on the stem represented events in my life, and I was trying to create a visual timeline. I could point to the beads and tell you what each one represents. There is a chronological order to my bead timeline. But then I turned the stem around, looking straight down the end, with all the beads aligned. From this perspective, I could no longer see all the individual beads, yet I knew they were still there. The order of the beads was no longer visible.

I think maybe God has this kind of timeless perspective. If what we are praying for happens tomorrow, or not for twenty years, the bead will still be on the stem. We want what we pray for *now*. God wants to answer our prayers in his timing for reasons we can't always understand.

Sometimes we get a glimpse of the purpose of the wait to help us understand God's amazing timing. A woman my Dad knew from his prison ministry had been incarcerated for many years. Tammy had come to know Jesus in prison, and studied the Bible, hungry to grow in her faith. She used what little money she had to order books and Bible study aids. When her book order came, it sat in the prison warehouse for months. Tammy knew the books had arrived, and was crushed that no one would bring them to her.

Months went by until one night, a guard came and escorted her to the warehouse to finally get her books. As Tammy and the guard began to head back to her cell, Fourth of July fireworks filled the sky. Tammy stared in awe. She hadn't seen fireworks for over twenty years. The guard told her she could walk as slowly as she wanted, so she could enjoy them. The long wait for her books had provided a special gift that she would never forget.

Sometimes, when we are waiting, we need to remember God's record of faithfulness. Last year, when I was sulking from a rejection letter for my script, I revisited my personal journal. As I read and reminisced about the last few years, I could see many answered prayers, as well as ways God had blessed me in unexpected ways. I realized how quickly we forget his faithfulness. I think we need to reflect on his graciousness often when we are in a time of waiting.

In Deuteronomy Chapter 8, Moses prompts the Israelites to remember all that God has done for them. He warns them that when they are blessed with good land and abundant food and resources, it will be easy for them to forget the Lord God, and take the credit for their own success. Like the Israelites, we need to remember with humble hearts, that *all* that is good in our life comes from our Father God.

The Israelites often built things like wells and altars at the places where God had done something great. They did this so they would not forget what God had done, and they could tell the stories of his faithfulness for generations to come.

My Bible study group started filling a jar with marbles so we would remember how God answered our prayers. We call it our "Altar of Gratitude." Every time someone has a prayer answered, they add a marble to the jar. When I'm waiting a long time for prayers to be answered, when time is moving as slow as molasses in January, I look at all those marbles in the jar, and I remember how good and faithful he is.

In my strongest moments, when I'm looking straight at Jesus and ignoring the clocks and the calendars, I can sometimes have gratitude for prayers that haven't even been answered yet. When I step out of this chronological mindset, and give thanks now for what has yet to be manifested on my timeline, I think the timeless God must surely smile.

Group discussion questions:

1. Have you prayed for something that you had to wait painfully long for? Have you ever given up praying for something?

2. Are some prayers and dreams harder to have faith for? Why? 3. Is God powerful enough to answer your toughest prayers?

4. What would help you remember the answered prayers and ways God has blessed you?

Read and discuss these scripture passages:

James 5:7-8

Galatians 6:9

Philippians 1:6

Romans 5:3-4

Psalms 13

Psalms 130:5-6

Isaiah 30:18

The Great I Am

I am the alpha and omega, says the
Lord God, "Who is, and who was,
and who is to come, the almighty."
Revelation 1:8

Over the two years I have been working on writing this, I have heard, read, and noticed many things about the subject of time. This often happens when our attention focuses on something. Our brains create a new category for the topic de jour. This *Frequency Illusion*[10] causes us to notice things that would have been previously ignored or overlooked.

While writing this, I began to notice the plethora of songs written about time and the struggles with time. My original draft had quotes from some of the many lyrics about time I came across. Then I researched what the permissions to incorporate these lyrics would cost me. Yikes! So in my second draft, they all got cut.

I read C.S. Lewis's book, *Mere Christianity,*[11] many years ago, but I didn't remember the chapter *Time and Beyond Time* in the last section of the book. Maybe I took the author's advice at the beginning of the chapter that some readers should skip over this part of the book, as it might be an *unnecessary complication*. Of course now, it was the part I turned to first. In this theological classic, published in 1952, Lewis suggests that some of our difficulty in accepting the vastness of God and his capabilities is that we comprehend him in the backdrop of our reference of time.

He suggests if we picture time as a straight line that we travel, then we must picture God as the whole page on which that line is drawn. He goes on to describe how the understanding of a God who can see all...past, present, and future, should not interfere with the idea that we have free will. He explains God does not "foresee" what you will do tomorrow, he simply sees what you will you do, because he knows tomorrow as he knows every day.

While I have come to a better understanding of how God is outside of time, I also see more clearly how time is governed by his omnipotence.

I recently watched a miniseries about the life of Einstein. Einstein turned things up-side-down when he challenged the current accepted idea that time was absolute. His theories of relativity explained how time was connected to space and therefore relative.

The understanding that time is relative means one thing in science, and another in our experiential perspectives. Our perception of time is that it is relative to our circumstances. For the person who has been told they have six months to live, every hour seems to evaporate with the brutal awareness that each remaining hour is becoming more endangered. But across town, another person sits in a prison cell aching for time to pass quickly. When he puts a big X across the date on the calendar, it is a day that he never wants to see again.

But by drawing close to the Creator of time, the person living with limited days can embrace the hours made precious with his presence. And the person trapped in misery can also draw close to the holy one who will sustain him. I think we must trust God that there is a right time for everything.

So while I accept the scientific principal that time is not absolute, but relative, I also believe that time is *subject.* The Creator of time has dominion over it. If space can make time behave differently, then surely time is subject to the authority of the one who spoke space and time into existence.

I recently attended a healing service where the minister said he believed that God could take your body back to the point in time before it became ill, or he could accelerate the body's healing by taking it to the point in the future where it is fully restored. This time travel view of God's power may be too much for you, but I stopped thinking *"God can't do that,"* long ago. My God is supernatural and he is in every moment of time. He has dominion over time, because time is his creation.

Almost every believer I know has a story about God's timing, and how it affected their life. I have had moments where a friend came to my mind and after I prayed for her, I found out later why she came to my mind at that specific time. I also know that when I have put my busy agenda on hold to spend quiet time with God, somehow my day seemed to stretch wider and longer, and I accomplished even more than I anticipated.

While our Father God has always existed and has no beginning, there was a beginning to time. Science tells us that time is duration that marks change, and change is the proof that time has passed. Physics also tells us that time exists only when matter exists. Since God is spirit *(John 4:24)* and he never changes *(Malachi 3:6, James 1:17)*, it stands to reason that time was not required until God created a physical universe. I think the gift of time, and with it the opportunity for change, were essential for our free will.

We make dozens of choices every day, including how we use our time. At the end of the day, I reflect on this daily gift of 1440 minutes. How many of these did I spend with the Creator who gave me this day? Did I use any of this gift of time to bring a smile to someone's face? How am I spending the days that are represented by the dash between my birth and death date? In Paul's letter to the Philippians, he encourages us to "Shine like stars in the sky." *(Philippians 2:15)* Did I shine today? Was I even for a few moments the *Salt of the Earth* or the *Light of the World* that I am called to be? *(Matt. 5:13-16)* If *change* is the outcome of time passed, what does that change look like in my life today?

Not only do we make choices with how we use the time God gives us, we decide the quality of our participation in that time. Do I juggle my attention halfheartedly in an attempt to do more than is humanly possible? Sometimes I feel like a human Swiss army knife: trying to be all things to all people.

My focus may be on something monumental or ordinary, but whatever it is, I want to try and do it with all my heart. Is my love for my Savior reflected in everything that I set my hands and mind to?

I think these are questions I will struggle with daily. There is no *there,* there, but I can move forward. Will I waste time today? Most certainly. I'm currently entertaining thoughts that I may have wasted months and even years with my lofty goals of writing movie scripts. Yesterday I got the annual contest rejection letter, and today I am questioning my sanity and wondering if I should put this dream to bed. It definitely calls for time to reflect and seek God's wisdom. I'm thinking about Solomon's advice in Ecclesiastes 3: *There is a time for everything....A time to keep and a time to throw away.*

But then the words of Brother Lawrence come to my mind: *"...He isn't impressed so much with the dimensions of our work, as with the love in which it is done."* My stories were works of love for sure, and in the writing process, I was changed. I want to believe that there is another purpose beyond this, but apparently this isn't the kairos time for my stories. I take comfort though, in that Solomon also proclaimed in Ecclesiastes, *"He has made everything beautiful in its time." (3:11)* Like yeast in bread, sometimes there are unseen transformations that just can't be rushed.

In seven days I am back to teaching, and my writing time will become a rare luxury. Will I be able to practice what I have learned when I face the demands of teaching and have an agenda full of meetings? *Be still. Reflect. Seize. Breathe, Selah, Listen.* Even in the laid back recess of summer it was a challenge for me.

When I started writing this, I began to notice how often people mention time. I frequently heard people say, *"I just don't have time."* or *"We didn't have enough time."* I even heard, *"There's not enough time in the day."* The comments were almost always stated as a deficit, or with a negative perspective. And there's also the multitude of songs written over the years about our conflicted relationship with time. Do we really believe God's gift to us is insufficient?

Like Solomon concludes in Ecclesiastes, we can choose to focus on how short life is and question the meaning of life, or we can find joy in each day and satisfaction in our work and all we do. Do we see time with boundaries like a hostile barbed wire fence, or do we see it as the green pasture within?

Is your "hour" glass half empty or half full? Remember the threatening hourglass in the *Wizard of Oz*[12] passing red sand as Dorothy awaited her fate? Sometimes I see time that way. Gravity is pulling the sand down the hour glass way too fast. I know my focus on the passage of time clouds my vision of the sacred value of each moment.

I often think about when Peter walked on the water with Jesus. *(Matt 14:22-33)* When Peter looked straight at Jesus, he walked confidently on the water towards him, but when he began to focus on the wind and the waves, he started to sink. When I experience weakness and doubt, I ask myself what I am looking at. My wind and waves are often the circumstances, and sometimes the watch on my wrist. I need to turn my eyes to Jesus. I think our perception of time could be altered if we would only focus on the time giver, instead of the clock on the wall.

At the end of the day, do I reflect on what I didn't get done or can I smile thinking of the moments I was able to steal away to meet in secret with the lover of my soul? Maybe I used five whole minutes to enjoy eating an orange, singly focused on the fragrance and taste. Maybe I turned off the T.V. or put aside my phone and sat in the quiet to just listen for a few minutes. Or maybe I just have to end my day by falling asleep with a few deep breaths while I whisper, *"Abba, I am yours."*

Time has been measured and contemplated throughout history. Yet no powerful kingdom, advanced civilization, or modern advancement in technology has been able to master or control it.

Wealth can be accumulated, given, or inherited; matter can be manipulated, recycled, or transformed; even less tangible things like love can grow, be shared and received, and remain after death. But time is transient and totally ungovernable.

Each second that passes will never exist again. Time has a value that cannot be quantified. The great and timeless "I Am" gave us eternal souls, but temporary bodies that must submit to the parameters of time. We think about time a lot, but we rarely think about it as the unique and precious gift that it is.

Time is a great reminder of God's grace. We may misuse or squander time, yet each new day there is a new gift. I pray that our eyes are opened to see time as the gift that it is and to value and embrace each moment. The Great "I Am" exists in every moment of every day, just waiting for us to turn our faces toward him.

We are free to choose how we spend our time, and though we often fail to make wise or holy choices, we are given a brand new gift each morning. His amazing supply of mercies keeps providing a new gift of time each day until he decides to replace this gift with the *ultimate gift* of timeless eternity.

Group discussion questions:
1. *Has your perspective of time changed? How?*
2. *What do you think you might do to help you embrace time as the gift from God that it is?*
3. *What goal(s) might you work towards? Here are a few ideas:*
   - *Identifying the time bandits in your life*
   - *Single tasking and doing whatever you do with all your heart*
   - *Taking time to reflect and breathe throughout your day*
   - *Prioritize your tasks and activities*
   - *Seize the kairos moments you may be overlooking*
   - *Spend sacred time in God's presence each day*
   - *Recognize time as a gift from God and respond in gratitude*

Read and discuss these scripture passages:
James 1:17
Lamentations 3:22-23
Matthew 5:13-16
Luke 6:38

The Totally Unexpected
Gift of Time

"Come to me, all you who are weary
and burdened, and I will give you
rest. Take my yoke upon you and
learn from me, for I am gentle and
humble in heart, and you will find
rest for your souls."
Matthew 11: 28-29

I can hear the birds singing. I turn off the T.V. and go outside to hear them better. *If you can still hear birds, there is hope.* The President is speaking to the nation again, now a daily occurrence. It is March 30, 2020, and the world is in crisis due to the Corona virus. In a few weeks our lives have changed radically.

It started with a few events cancelling. I felt inconvenienced. I had been looking forward to the Saint Patrick's Festival. Then suddenly, schools, churches, gyms, and restaurants closed. Things accelerated by the day. Many people were out of work. Store shelves emptied. Many states had shelter-in-place orders and some countries in the world were in full lockdown. What is happening? So many questions. How long will this last? How bad is this? Today I cried along with other teachers when we found out that we will not return to school this schoolyear. This feels like a dream.

But outside, the birds are still singing. I think of the scripture from Matthew 6:

Look at the birds of the air; they do
not sow or reap or store away in
barns, and yet your heavenly Father
feeds them. Are you not much more

valuable than they? Can any one of
you by worrying add a single hour to
your life?

Suddenly, we have lots of time on our hands. All the things I filled my hours with are fading away. There are still many people working very hard and long hours....medical staff, grocery workers, truckers, police, and first responders. We are *so thankful* for them. While we quarantine in our homes, they are out there keeping us safe and alive.

But all the extracurricular activities are gone. We don't go to the gym, or movies, social gatherings, or even church. The only shopping is for food, and it looks very different. I went out to Trader Joes yesterday and waited in a line of people six feet apart as ten people were let into the store at a time.

"Come to me," He says.

"I'm here for you. Let's sit outside
and listen to the birds and enjoy the
flowers. You can bring that book
you've been too busy to read. And
we'll catch up. I love to listen to you
tell me what's on your heart. And I
have things to share with you too."

I have been bouncing from television news, to Facebook, to email. We're in a crisis. The news is changing by the day. I try to digest all I'm hearing. Then I check in on family and friends through phone and Facebook. The comic relief and memes lighten my spirits. Songs and scriptures are shared. We watch sequestered Italians join in song from their balconies. *We will get through this.*

A few days in it hits me. This is an *unexpected* gift of time. This is our chance to hit the reset button. To clear out the clutter that filled our hours. A time to reassess what is really important. To spend time with family, to sit at the feet of Papa God. I had the will, but not the willpower to do this on my own. God has cleared my calendar for me.

Now, I'm not saying God smote the world with this virus, but he is sovereign and it's evident he is allowing it to happen. One of my Pastors, Mark Buckley shared his belief that God is calling a *time out* to help us refocus. He reminded us that God disciplines those he loves. Hebrews 12:10 says *"God disciplines us for our good in order that we may share his holiness."* Our Pastor David Stockton reminded us that God uses the temporal world and the challenges we go through to produce in us something everlasting.

After I wrote and published this book, *The Gift of Time,* I heard feedback from those who read it that it definitely struck a familiar chord. I wasn't the only one who felt the demands on my time were out of hand. And self-reflection revealed that a lot of the turbulence we were experiencing was of our own making. I began to notice sermons, devotions, songs, and other books that revealed to me that many other people were arriving at the same insights. My pastor spoke of a book titled, *The Ruthless Elimination of Hurry,* by John Mark Comer, and I found myself reading *Present Over Perfect,* by Shauna Niequist. It seemed to be everywhere…this cry for us to slow down, reassess, let go, and breathe.

I think God heard our hearts. And like the good father that he is, he wants the best for us too. We have experienced the brakes being applied to our *way over the speed limit* lives. And at this slower speed, we are now able to see the view of the beauty around us that we missed in the blur of our ever accelerating lives. Things we took for granted have suddenly become very precious.

In times like these we are humbled. We are reminded that we are not as self-sufficient as we thought. We have falsely believed that as Americans we are always safe, and we can fix anything that infringes on our comfort and freedom. We now have a choice to strengthen our faith and live day to day, or succumb to the fear that grows as we experience less and less control over our lives.

We see the effects of fear when we see the empty shelves at the grocery store. We see the effects of fear when we hear that gun and ammo sales are soaring. But we also see faith and kindness growing every day. People sharing what they have. Companies redesigning their production to help out. We see fashion designers making face masks, breweries making hand sanitizer, and automakers and vacuum makers making ventilators. A crisis can bring out our best if we let it. Similar stories of selflessness and generosity happened after 9/11, and probably every time that the reset button has been pushed in history.

In the last weeks, I've had my moments where fear invaded my psyche. But faith is the spiritual muscle that develops if we push against fear. Muscles won't develop unless you lift some weights and experience some resistance. Muscle hypertrophy actually occurs when the fibers of the muscles sustain damage or injury. The body repairs the damaged fibers by fusing them, which increases the mass and size of the muscles. So don't feel defeated if you feel some fear. Just push against it. Push against it with the words and promises of God.

When I see the empty shelves at the store, or hear the death stats on the news, or read the updates that seem to come hourly, I need to push against fear by embracing this gift of time that God has given us and honoring it by drawing closer to him.

I wonder how this will feel when it is a memory from long ago. I want to write about this now so I remember this time. How we began to conserve toilet paper, and share basic supplies with others. I don't want to forget how the things we took for granted suddenly became very precious to us. How we missed gathering with friends, or longed to just hug someone again.

In Exodus 16, the Israelites who had been freed from Egypt were facing starvation in the desert. Through Moses, God promised that manna would rain down from the skies each day. They were instructed to take only what they needed for that day. God was teaching them trust. Trust that he would provide....day by day. Just like our current experience with toilet paper and food, some people stockpiled that manna. But it immediately rotted, because they didn't trust in God's provision. There is much to learn from this story. But what I want to focus on, is God's command that they preserve a jar of the manna for future generations to remember how they had been provided for.

I think God knows how quickly we forget. I keep hearing people say, *"When things get back to normal."* Our prayer is that this virus will be beat, and that it will be safe to gather together again. But maybe there is a better place than *back to normal*. Maybe when we are free to plan our lives again, we don't need to fill the calendar so full. Maybe we will remember how we learned to value how we spend our time and realized what was really important. Maybe we need to put some symbolic manna in a jar to put on our shelf to remind us of how God provided for us and taught us what is really important.

I wonder how the children of today will tell stories of this time to their children. What would we put in a time capsule from 2020? When the children of 2020 are young adults, some believe they will look back on this time as the most precious time of their lives. Why? Because their family started eating together again and spending time together. They played board games and laughed as Mom and Dad tried to fill in as their teacher. Because suddenly life was pared down to a simplicity that seemed better in many ways. And families drew close and loved each other harder.

So maybe we don't want to return to *normal*. Maybe the gift of time will be more precious than ever.

Note: This chapter was added eight months after this book was originally published.

Notes:

[1] Mitch Albom, *The Time Keeper,* New York: 2012

[2] Sophie Bates, Stanford News, *A decade of data reveals that heavy multitaskers have reduced memory, Stanford Psychologist says,* Re: research of: Clifford Nass, Anthony Wagner, and Melina Uncapher.

[3] Kirstin Fawcett, *Why Multitasking is Bad for your Brain,* February 4, 2016

[4] Brother Lawrence, *The Practice of the Presence of God,* 1692.

[5] Frank C. Laubach, *Letters by a Modern Mystic,* Edited and compiled by Constance E. Padwick. Syracuse, N.Y.: New Readers Press, 1955. First published in 1937.

[6] Frank C. Laubach, *The Game with Minutes.* First published in 1956.

[7] *Mother Teresa: Come Be My Light: The Private Writings of the Saint of Calcutta,* By Brian Kolodiejchuk, Editor, Doubleday Religion, 2007.

[8] *Dead Poets Society,* Written by: Tom Schulman, Producer: Touchstone pictures, Director: Peter Weir, USA, 1989.

[9] *Gone With the Wind,* Adapted from the Novel by Margaret Mitchell, Screenplay by Sidney Howard, Producer: David O. Selznick, Director: Victor Fleming, USA, 1939.

[10] The Frequency Illusion is also known as the Baader-Meinhoff Phenomenon. I refrained myself from elaborating because I probably would have rambled on too long.

[11] *Mere Christianity,* By C.S. Lewis, Publisher: Geoffrey Bles, 1952.

[12] *The Wizard of Oz,* Adapted from L. Frank Baum's: The Wonderful Wizard of Oz, Director: Victor Fleming, Producer: Mervyn LeRoy, USA, 1939.

My Gift of Time

Thank you to my husband, Jerry Crow, for designing the beautiful cover. This visual helps us remember where our gift of time comes from.

I kept this book short – appropriate for people who struggle with time management. Now I ask for your grace. I've never published before, so I'm sure I've made a few mistakes.

I want this book to be a gift of my time so I will keep the cost as low as I am able to. My goal is to share in a growth journey with others in understanding God's gift of time.

Please share this with friends and study groups who may also desire to embrace time as the special gift that it is. A very special gift of your time would be to write a review of the book on Amazon.

Made in the USA
Las Vegas, NV
15 September 2021